Juan José Warner, Benjamin Ignatius Hayes, Joseph Pomeroy
Widney

An Historical Sketch of Los Angeles County, California

Juan José Warner, Benjamin Ignatius Hayes, Joseph Pomeroy Widney

An Historical Sketch of Los Angeles County, California

ISBN/EAN: 9783744669597

Printed in Europe, USA, Canada, Australia, Japan

Cover: Foto ©ninafisch / pixelio.de

More available books at **www.hansebooks.com**

AN

HISTORICAL SKETCH

— OF —

LOS ANGELES COUNTY,

CALIFORNIA.

———✳———

From the Spanish occupancy, by the Founding of the Mission San Gabriel Archangel, September 8, 1771, to July 4, 1876.

———✳———

PUBLISHED BY

LOUIS LEWIN & Co.,

No. 14 Spring Street.

———◦—

LOS ANGELES, CAL.:
MIRROR PRINTING, RULING AND BINDING HOUSE.

1876.

INTRODUCTORY.

To the Literary Committee of the Los Angeles Centennial Celebration :

GENTLEMEN : We, the Committee appointed by you to prepare an Historical Review of Los Angeles City and County, from the earliest settlement to the present time, have prepared, and present to you this sketch. The field has been so extensive—embracing a period of more than a century—that we have been necessarily forced to pass over the ground hastily, and no doubt have omitted much of interest; yet, so far as in our power lies, we have endeavored to make the sketch worthy of the subject and of the occasion. Drawing our information from many sources, some of it recorded, but much unrecorded, narratives and personal reminiscences falling directly from the lips of survivors of that older generation, now rapidly passing away—persons who in recounting these tales of the past, may with pride, like Æneas, say "et quorum pars magna fui," we have sifted and compared reports and dates, until we believe the narrative will be found in the main correct.

If this sketch meet your approval and the approbation of the public, and if it should be the instrument of rescuing from oblivion a portion of the early history of our country, and, especially, if it may be the means of adding only one more tie to the bond that makes us, of whatever blood or kin, citizens of one common home, brothers by adoption, children of one fatherland, we shall feel that our labor has been amply repaid.

J. J. WARNER, ⎫
BENJ. HAYES, ⎬ Committee.
J. P. WIDNEY, ⎭

LOS ANGELES, July 4th, 1876.

CENTENNIAL HISTORY.

——✠——

CHAPTER I.

LOS ANGELES COUNTY FROM SEPTEMBER 8TH, 1771, TO AUGUST, 1846

OS ANGELES COUNTY includes within its present bounda-ries the sites of three Roman Catholic Missions, which were founded in the following order, and named San Gabriel Archangel, September 8th, 1771, San Juan Capistrano, in 1776, and San Fernando, in 1797. The Mission of San Gabriel was at first planted on the margin of the San Gabriel River, some four or five miles southeasterly from its present site. This river had previously received the name of "*Temblores*" (earthquakes), from the missionaries or the soldiers who had traveled over the country from San Diego to Monterey. No exten-sive or permanent improvements were made at that place, and it was not long before its present site was selected. The Mission of San Juan Capistrano was also at first located some miles northeasterly from the present location, and at the foot of the mountain. The place of its first location is still known, as is also that of San Gabriel, as *La Mision Vieja* (old Mission). The founders of these missions, as well as those of all the twenty-one missions established within the limits of the State of California, were natives of Spain, and Friars of the Order of San Francisco, and were sent to the field of their labors by the College of San Fernando, in the City of Mexico, which college belonged to the Franciscan Order of Friars.

The unbroken series of failures, which for more than one hundred and fifty years attended the oft recurring attempts of the civil and military power of New Spain, supplemented by a number of individual efforts by men of wealth and power, to reduce the natives of Peninsular California to the domination of Spain, to convert them to Christianity, to found colonies and establish military posts among them, as well as the barrenness of the country itself, caused the Government of New Spain to abandon an enterprise which was undertaken in 1534 by the conqueror of Mexico, Hernando Cortez, in person.

While contemplating—about 1690—its withdrawal from any further effort for the reduction of California, the Government of New Spain submitted to the Society of Jesuits—an Order of the Roman Catholic Church—proposals for the subjugation and conversion to Christianity of the natives, and the consequent extension of Spanish authority over the people and country of Peninsular California by that Society.

The proposals were accepted, and the first few missionaries (accompanied by five soldiers and a commanding officer, furnished by the government), sent forth by that Society, to accomplish a work which had alike baffled the power of the Government of New Spain and individual efforts, landed on the eastern shore of the Peninsula in 1697. In the space of forty-eight years from the time the pioneers of this religious enterprise stepped upon the shores of this sterile land, fourteen prosperous missions were established throughout the Peninsula, and the whole Indian population, a small portion of which, inhabiting its eastern shore. had successfully withstood the attacks of the military forces of the Government of New Spain, were reduced to the control of the Jesuit Missionaries, and subjection to the Spanish power.

The success which crowned the labors of the Jesuit Missionaries in Peninsular California, stimulated the Franciscan Order of the Roman Catholic Church in Mexico, to attempt a like work along the shore of the Pacific Ocean from the Peninsula northerly. This enterprise was approved of and assisted by the Government of New Spain, and was also fostered and encouraged by zealous Christians and philanthropists of Mexico, who donated large sums of money and estates to aid in its prosecution.

The first expedition, sent to this new field of labor by the College of San Fernando, was in three detachments—two of which were to proceed up by land over the Peninsula, and the other, in three vessels, to go by water. Each detachment was accompanied by a small military force, which force numbered, in all, four companies. That portion of the expedition which went by water, embarked at San Blas, and, after calling at Loreto, a peninsular port, sailed from thence for San Diego and Monterey. These vessels, the San Carlos, the San Antonio, and the San Joseph, were the transports of the detachment sent by water. Two of these vessels, called packet boats, only reached San Diego; the other, the San Joseph, was never heard from after leaving Loreto. The San Antonio arrived at San Diego on the 11th of April, and the San Carlos on the 1st of May, 1769. The two detachments by land reached San Diego, one May 14th, and the other July 1st, of the same year. The land detachments brought two hundred head of neat cattle, a number of horses and mares, sheep, goats, and hogs, with which to stock the country they were on their way to subdue and occupy.

The Missionary Friars were under the control of a President, who directed when and where a mission should be established, and designated the Friar or Friars that should have charge of it. The President was appointed by the Principal of the College, or Convent, of San Fernando, and was himself a Friar, and came to California with the first expedition. He had the general supervision of the missions, and changed the resident Friars from mission to mission as his judgment dictated.

The commander of the military force which accompanied these Missionaries was Gaspar de Portala, a captain of cavalry, who was appointed Governor of California by the Viceroy of New Spain, and he and his successors for many years held the offices of Governor and Commanding General of California.

It was not contemplated, either by the Government of New Spain or the Directory of the College of San Fernando, that the missions to be established should remain permanently as missions, but that at the expiration of ten years from the founding of each and every mission, it should be converted into a municipal organization, known as a Pueblo, and that the property created and acquired by the mission, during the term of its continuance, should vest in the inhabitants of the political organization. It soon became evident, to both the ecclesiastic and political authorities, that at the end of the ten years the neophytes of a mission—the converted Indians—would be incompetent to form a political organization, or to rightly use and manage the property accumulated by the mission; and, consequently, no steps were taken while California was subject to Spain, nor for more than fifty years after the establishment of the first mission in California, to convert them into Pueblos.

In less than sixty years from the founding of the Mission of San Gabriel, the herds of neat cattle, bands of horses, and flocks of sheep and goats, of the three missions of this county, covered the major part of the land in Los Angeles County, and all that part of San Bernardino County lying south and west of the San Bernardino Mountain Range. The number of Indian converts in these three missions was, in 1802, two thousand six hundred and seventy-four. In 1831, when these missions had reached their highest prosperity, the number of neophytes was more than four thousands. By the labor of the subjugated and converted Indians the missionaries planted orchards and vineyards, and cultivated large fields of corn, wheat, barley, beans and other food vegetables. As soon after the founding of a mission as its circumstances would permit, a large pile of buildings in the form of a quadrangle, composed in part of burnt brick, but chiefly of sun-dried ones, was erected around a spacious court. A large and capacious church, which usually occupied one of the outer corners of the quadrangle, was a necessary and conspicuous part of the pile. In this massive building, covered with red tile, was the habitation of the Friar, rooms for guests, and for the majordomos and their families, hospital wards, store-houses and granaries, rooms for the carding, spinning, and weaving of woolen fabrics, shops for blacksmiths, joiners and carpenters, saddlers, shoemakers, and soap-boilers, and cellars for storing the product (wine and brandy) of the vineyards. Near the habitation of the Friar, and in front of the large building, another building, of similar materials was placed and used as quarters for a small number—about a corporal's guard—of soldiers, under command of a non-commissioned officer, to hold the Indian neophytes in check, as well as to protect the mission from the attacks of hostile Indians. The soldiers at each mission also acted as couriers, carrying from mission to mission the correspondence of the government officers and the Friars. These small detachments of soldiers, which were stationed at each mission, were furnished by one or the other of the military posts at San Diego or Santa Barbara, both of which were military garrisons. At an early period in the history of San Gabriel, a water-power mill, for grinding wheat, was constructed and put in operation in front of and near the mission building. At a later period, a new grist mill was built by the mission, and placed about two miles west of the mission proper. This was also operated by water-power. The building in which was placed this mill now forms a part of the residence of E. J. C. Kewen, Esq. A water-power saw mill was also built by this mission, and was located near the last mentioned grist mill. These were the only mills made or, used in California, either for grinding or sawing, in which water was the motive power, or in which a wheel was used, for more than half a century after the founding of the first mission in continental California. In these two grist mills the revolving mill stone was upon the upper end of a vertical shaft, and the water-wheel upon the lower end, so that the revolution of the stone was no more frequent than that of the water-wheel.

In 1831, the minister at San Gabriel, Friar Sanchez, aided and encouraged Wm. Wolfskill, Nathaniel Prior, Richard Laughlin, Samuel Prentice, and George Yount (all Americans), to build a schooner at San Pedro, which was employed, by the Americans named, in the hunting of sea otter. The same year, or in the preceding year, Friar Sanchez purchased a brig which was employed in commerce between this coast and the ports of Mexico and South America.

Of the products or manufactures of those missions, during the sovereignty of Spain over California, very little was exported, being mostly consumed by those who belonged to the mission or by the inhabitants of the Town of Los Angeles, and the stock breeders in the country adjacent.

Such was the patience, the energy, the business capacity, and tact with which the Friars controlled and managed the Indians, and the general affairs of the missions, that in a few years, with some supplies which—while the power of Spain was undisturbed in Mexico—were annually sent them from the Port of San Blas, by their Convent in the City of Mexico, their granaries and storehouses were filled to overflowing, and the intervening country, from mission to mission, was covered with live stock, and their shepherds and herders were counted by hundreds. Although in the annual lists of stock and of agricultural products made out by the Friars, the number was much less, it was estimated by the most competent judges that the number of neat cattle belonging to the three missions, in 1831, exceeded one hundred thousand, with sheep and horse kind in full proportion.

After the independence of Mexico, 1821, the discharged soldiers and their offspring, who desired to obtain land upon which to breed cattle, began to agitate the matter of the conversion of the missions into towns, and in 1824, the Mexican Congress enacted a law under which, in 1828, the Executive of the Mexican Government issued regulations for the disposal of the public lands. The conversion of the missions into towns did not meet with the approbation and hearty approval of the Friars in charge of the missions, and the transition was so slow, and attended with so many obstacles, that only the Mission of San Juan Capistrano reached the condition of being dressed in the swaddling clothes of a political organization. The control and management of the neophytes, and the temporalities of the missions, were taken from the Friars about 1835 and given to secular officers, called administrators, who were appointed by the Governor of California.

When the Friars became convinced that the conversion of the missions into towns was determined upon by the Mexican Government, the prudent and economical management of the missions, which hitherto had been the practice, became, during the last few years in which they were under their control, wasteful. Under the far more improvident management of the secular officers, the personal effects of the missions rapidly diminished, and those buildings, which had been reared by the toil and labor of thousands of Indian converts, and which had so heavily taxed the powers of the Friars, and had been their pride and their glory, were not long in giving evidence of neglect. The artificial water courses, which had been constructed under the direction of the Friars, to conduct water to the gardens, orchards, fields, and vineyards, for irrigation, were neglected, their banks broken and rendered useless for the conveyance of water. The orchards and vineyards were left without irrigation or proper cultivation. Groves of olives were barbarously felled and converted into firewood. Fruit orchards and vineyards were left unprotected by fence from the inroads of cattle, until in 1846 hardly a vestige of the vines, which had covered scores of acres of land, was left remaining. The orange orchard of San Gabriel, and a fragment of the vineyard and olive grove of San Fernando, still remain, as living witnesses of the energy and untiring industry of those zealous Friars who, coming into a country full to overflowing with ignorant, savage barbarians, changed them into patient, docile laborers, and in less than fifty years filled the country with fruitfulness.

Subsequent to the establishment of the missions, and before the close of that century, the Spanish Government, acting through the commanding officer of California, did, at different periods of time, grant four large tracts of land lying in this county for private individuals. The area of these tracts was from ten to twenty, or more, square leagues each. They were granted to the following persons, who had come to California as soldiers, and who had been discharged or retired from active service on account of their age or other causes. The Nietos Tract, embracing all the land between the Santa Ana and San Gabriel Rivers, and from the sea to and including some of the hill land on its northeastern frontier, was granted by Governor Pedro Fages to Manuel Nieto, in 1784. The Santiago de Santa Ana Tract, a large area lying along the Santa Ana River, on its easterly side, and extending from tide water to and some miles within the hill lands, was granted to Antonio Yorba in July, 1810. The San Rafael Tract, lying on the left bank of the Los Angeles River, and extending to the Arroyo Seco, was granted by Governor Pedro Fages October 20th, 1784, and the grant was reaffirmed by Governor Borica January 12th, 1798, to Jose Maria Verdugo. The San Pedro Tract, lying along the ocean, and the estuary of San Pedro, was granted to Juan Jose Dominguez by Pablo Vicente Sola, December 31st, 1822.

The dates of these grants are taken from "Hoffman's Reports of Land Cases," but some of the dates are undoubtedly erroneous. This " Report of

Land Cases " says the grant to Antonio Yorba was made by José Figueroa July 1st, 1810. The only Figueroa who held the office of Governor of California, or who in the whole history of California issued grants of lands, was General Jose Figueroa, who was appointed in April, 1832, and reached Monterey, California—having come by water—in January, 1833. Consequently, he could not have made a grant of land in California in 1810. There is much circumstancial testimony tending to show that both the Yorba and Dominguez grants were made during the past century. Antonio Maria Lugo, a prominent citizen of Los Angeles, giving testimony in the District Court, at Los Angeles, in 1857, said his age was seventy-six years; that he remembered the Pueblo of Los Angeles as early as 1785. That he had known the Verdugo, or San Rafael Ranch, since 1790. That Verdugo had had his ranch since 1784, and that it, "San Rafael," was the third oldest ranch in the county—the Nietos and the Dominguez being the oldest. During the first quarter of the present century, the Santiago de Santa Ana Ranch was universally known, among the people inhabiting this county, as one of the oldest ranchos, and there are many good reasons for the belief that its founding was contemporary with that of San Rafael. There is no room to doubt the statement that a grant of the Santiago de Santa Ana Tract, to Jose Antonio Yorba, was made in 1810 by Jose Joaquin de Arrillaga, but in a partition suit in the District Court, for this county, a few years ago, for the partition of that tract of land among the heirs and claimants, testimony was introduced which showed that the original occupant of that tract was N. Grijalva, who, as also his wife, died, leaving only two children, both daughters. That one of these daughters married Jose Antonio Yorba, and the other Juan Pablo Peralta, and it is far more probable that the former of these two latter persons obtained a new or confirmed grant from Arrillaga, in 1810, than that Grijalva should have established himself upon the tract without having obtained a grant from the Governor. As Governor Borica, in 1798, issued to Jose Maria Verdugo a new or confirmatory grant of the Tract of San Rafael, which had been granted to Verdugo by Governor Fages, in 1784, so it is probable that the first title papers for San Pedro and Santiago de Santa Ana had disappeared, or were not presented to the United States Land Commissions for California. In this partition suit the Court recognized the claim of the Peraltas as descendants of the original proprietor of the land. Don Manuel Dominguez, one of the present proprietors of the San Pedro Ranch, states positively that the grant of that tract was made in 1784.

The Friars abstained, and the owners of live stock were prohibited by the government, from killing any female animals. This restraining policy had the effect of rapidly increasing the live stock of the country. The individuals, to whom the before mentioned grants of land were made, rapidly increased their live stock, so that before the termination of the first quarter of the present century, their almost boundless lands were covered with cattle and horses.

As early as 1825, the number of neat cattle and horse kind had increased so much, that the pasturage of the country embraced in this county was insufficient for its support, and that of the wild horses, of which there were tens of thousands which had no claimant, and which in small bands, each under its male leader, roamed over their respective haunts, consuming the herbage, and enticing into their bands the horses and brood mares of the stock breeders. To relieve themselves from these losses, the rancheros constructed large pens (corrals), with outspreading wings of long extent from the doorway, into which the wild horses were driven in large numbers and slaughtered. At a later period, and when the number of neat cattle had been somewhat lessened, the wild horses were driven into such pens and reduced to domestication.

The social and political history of this county, for the first half century or more, from the founding of the missions, are alike barren of any noticeable event. In the physical history, the most remarkable was the occurrence of an earthquake on the morning of the 8th of December, 1812. This day was the yearly feast day (la Purisima) of the Catholic Church, in commemoration of the immaculate conception of the Virgin Mary. The earthquake happened at the hour of the morning mass. The Church of the Mission of San Juañ Capistrano, a large stone building, which had been built but a few years (the roof of which was an arch, and of stone), in which were congregated a large number of the neophytes, was so severely shaken that the roof, except that portion over the transept, fell upon the worshipers, killing about thirty, and injuring a much larger number.

In 1825, the rivers of this county were so swollen that their beds, their banks, and the adjoining lands were greatly changed. At the date of the settlement of Los Angeles City, a large portion of the country, from the central part of the city to the tide water of the sea, through and over which the Los Angeles River now finds its way to the ocean, was largely covered with a forest, interspersed with tracts of marsh. From that time until 1825, it was seldom, if in any year, that the river discharged, even during the rainy season, its waters into the sea. Instead of having a river-way to the sea, the waters spread over the country, filling the depressions in the surface, and forming lakes, ponds, and marshes. The river water, if any, that reached the ocean, drained off from the land at so many places, and in such small volumes, that no channel existed until the flood of 1825, which, by cutting a river-way to tide water, drained the marsh land and caused the forests to disappear.

The flood of 1832 so changed the drainage, in the neighborhood of Compton and the northeastern portion of the San Pedro Ranch, that a number of lakes and ponds, covering a large area of the latter ranch, lying north and northwesterly from Wilmington, which to that date had been permanent, became dry in a few years thereafter. From 1825 until January, 1867, the San Gabriel and Los Angeles Rivers united at a point northerly from the dwelling house on the Cerritos Ranch, and flowing past the house on the west, emptied into the San Pedro estuary southwest of that dwelling house. The San Gabriel River, in the flood of 1867, left its bed at a point near where it struck the northern line of the Ranchito, and cut a new water-way through the central part of that ranch and the Santa Gertrudes and Alamitos Ranchos to the sea, east of the dwelling house on the latter ranch.

While statements respecting the existence of gold in the earth of California, and its procurement therefrom have been made and published as historical facts, carrying back the date of the knowledge of the auriferous character of this State as far as the time of the visit of Sir Francis Drake to this coast, there is no evidence to be found, in the written or oral history of the missions, the acts and correspondence of the civil or military officers, or in the unwritten and traditional history of Upper California, that the existence of gold, either with ores or in its virgin state, was ever suspected by any inhabitant of California previous to eighteen hundred and forty-one; and, furthermore, there is conclusive testimony that the first known grain of native gold dust was found upon or near the San Francisco Ranch, about forty-five miles westerly from Los Angeles City, in the month of June, 1841. This discovery consisted of grain gold fields—known as placer mines—and the auriferous fields, discovered in that year, embraced the greater part of the country drained by the Santa Clara River, from a point some fifteen or twenty miles from its mouth to its sources, and easterly beyond them to Mount San Bernardino.

The working of these fields has been pursued intermittingly, more or less successfully, from their discovery to the present time. The small supply of water, available for hydraulic mining over this large field, is the cause why it has not been more thoroughly worked. Although in no part of this extensive gold field have claims of great richness been found, a large number have been, and some are yet, worked with remunerating results.

The discovery of this gold field was, in a two-fold manner, accidental. Sometime in the latter part of 1840, or the early part of 1841, a Mexican mineralogist, Don Andres Castillero, traveling from Los Angeles to Monterey, while passing along the road over the Las Virgenes Rancho, saw and gathered up some small, water-worn mineralogical pebbles, known by Mexican placer miners as *tepustete*—a variety of pyrites—which he exhibited at the residence of Don Jose Antonio de la Guerra y Noriega, in Santa Barbara, where he was a guest, and stated, that wherever these pebbles were found in place, it was a good indication of placer gold fields. A Mr. Francisco Lopez, also known by the name of Cuso, a farmer and herdsman, living at the time upon the Piru Rancho, was present, and heard the statement and saw the pebbles. Not long after this incident, Mr. Lopez, in company with a fellow-herdsman, was one day searching for strayed animals until their riding horses were jaded. At a suitable place they dismounted, and picketing their horses that they might rest and feed, Lopez busied himself in gathering a parcel of wild onions, a bed of which was near at hand, to carry home for a mess of greens. In pulling the onions from the ground he noticed a pebble, similar to the one he had seen in the hands of Mr. Castillero, and remembering what was then said about its being a sign of gold, he scooped up a handful of the earth, which he had loosened by gathering the onions, and rubbing it in his hand, found a grain of gold.

The news of this discovery soon spread among the inhabitants, from Santa Barbara to Los Angeles, and in a few weeks hundreds of people were engaged in washing and winnowing the sands and earth of these gold fields. The writer of this visited the mines within a few weeks from their discovery, and from these mines was obtained the first parcel of California gold dust received at the United States Mint in Philadelphia, and which was sent to that mint by the Hon. Abel Stearns, late of Los Angeles City. It was sent with Alfred Robinson, and went in a merchant sailing ship around Cape Horn. A certificate of its deposit in the mint is in the possession of the Society of California Pioneers, in San Francisco.

Two parcels of placer gold—one from the New Mexican, and the other from the Sonorian gold fields—were brought to Los Angeles in the Winter of 1833–4, and were here sold and exported to foreign countries, which fact has served to cloud the history of gold discovery in California.

The Spanish Government, acting upon the ground that the people over whom it held sway, especially those of its subjects in America, were its wards, or incompetent persons, unable to make suitable provision for themselves, assumed the attitude of guardian toward its subjects. It ordained where and how they should live. It established the wages of laborers, and fixed the price of horses, cattle, and most commodities which were produced, or bought and sold by the people.

In consonance with this principle, the Town [Pueblo] of Nuestra Senora de Los Angeles, under and in conformity to an order of the then Governor of California, Phelipe de Neve, dated at the Mission of San Gabriel, August 26th, 1781, was founded in a formal manner on the fourth of September of the same year. The founders of the town numbered twelve adult males, all heads of families. The surnames of the twelve settlers were Lara, Navarro, Rosas, Mesa, Moreno, Rosas, Villaviccncia, Banegas, Rodriguez, Camero, Quintero, and Rodriguez. These men had been soldiers at the Mission of San Gabriel, and, although relieved or discharged from service, continued to receive pay and rations from the Spanish Government. The total number of souls comprising the settlement was forty-six. Twenty of these were children under ten years of age. Of the twelve adult men, two were natives of Spain, one a native of China, and the other nine of some one of the following places: Sinaloa, Sonora, and Lower California.

For the centre of the town a parallelogram, one hundred varas long and seventy-five wide, was laid out as a public square. Twelve house-lots, fronting on the square, occupied three sides of it, and one-half of the remaining side of seventy-five varas was destined for public buildings, and the other half an open space. The location of the public square would nearly correspond to the following lines: The southeast corner of Upper Main and Marchessault streets for the southern or southeastern corner of the square; the east line of Upper Main street, from the above named corner, one hundred varas in a northerly direction, for the east line of the square; the eastern line of New High street for the western line of the square; and the northern line of Marchessault street for the southern line of the square. At a short distance from the public square, and upon the alluvial bottom land of the river, upon which the water of the river for irrigation could be easily conducted, there were laid out thirty fields for cultivation. The fields contained forty thousand square varas each, and were mostly laid out in the form of a square, and separated from each other by narrow lanes. In accord with the paternal idea of the Spanish Government, the head of each family was furnished from the royal treasury with two oxen, two mules, two mares, two sheep, two goats, two cows with one calf, one ass, and one hoe, and to the settlers in common, the tools for a cart-maker. These articles, as well as the live stock, were all charged to the individuals respectively, or to the community at a price fixed by the Government, and the amount was to be deducted, in small installments, from their pay.

As the government of California was a combination of military and ecclesiastical powers, so the municipal government devised for the settlers of Los Angeles was a compound of political and military government, in which the latter largely predominated. All the municipal power was vested in one officer, called Alcalde, who was appointed by the Governor—who was himself the military commander of the country—or by a military officer who commanded the military district in which the town was situated. The territory of Upper California was divided into military districts corresponding in number with the military posts, which were four, and the jurisdiction of the commanding officer of the post extended over the district, and civil, as well as military matters, came under his cognizance.

The adult males, and those over eighteen years, were enrolled, and were subject to the performance of guard duty, both by day and night, at the guard house, which was located on the public square.

Notwithstanding that the laws of Spain, regarding the creation of towns or municipal organizations, were both munificent and liberal, yet as the organization of the municipal government of the Town of Los Angeles was effected by military officers exclusively, and as all those who composed the original settlers, as well as those who for many years became settlers, had been soldiers—trained and accustomed to military government and discipline—the evolution of the municipality from its military character, into a local self-governing community within its own sphere of action, was slow and tortuous. We find a military officer, one whose jurisdiction was co-extensive with that of the commanding officer of the garrison of Santa Barbara, granting a house-lot, in the Town of Los Angeles, on the 23d of June, 1821. This lot, upon which the Pico House stands, was granted to Jose Antonio Carrillo by his brother, Anastacio Carrillo, a military officer, who styled himself Commissioner. The exclusive jurisdiction of the *Alcalde*, the chief officer of Los Angeles, was extremely limited, even if in practice it was known to exist. Cases of all kinds, except such as could be heard by ecclesiastical authorities, both civil and criminal, and of trivial character, went from the Alcalde and beyond the territorial jurisdiction of Los Angeles, to be heard and determined by the military commandant of a garrison more than a hundred miles distant.

The absence of municipal records for the first half century after the founding of Los Angeles, of itself raises the presumption that the municipal officers exercised but little authority during that time. After the allotment of house lots and fields for cultivation to the original twelve settlers, there does not appear to have been any record kept of the grants of either house lots or farming lands until as late as 1836.

The system adopted by the Government for the formation of pueblos, and the granting of building lots and farming lands to settlers within the limits of a pueblo, did not require a record of the grant. In conferring upon a settler the right to acquire and occupy a lot upon which to build a dwelling house and land to cultivate, the Government did not absolutely divest itself of its title to and control over the soil. The settler who erected a house upon a lot assigned to him, or fenced and cultivated a field which had been set off to him, did not become vested with the unconditional title of ownership to either. If he, without justifiable cause, suffered his house to remain unoccupied, or to fall into decay, or his field to remain uncultivated for two consecutive years, it became subject to denouncement by any other person legally competent to take by grant, and the granting authorities could and were by law required, upon a proper showing of the abandonment, to grant the property to the informant, who then acquired the same and no better rights than those possessed by his predecessor.

Proof of the caution and circumspection necessary in collecting material for history, and the value of suspicion when directed to dates, is well exemplified by the following circumstance. We have before us a traced copy of the original order of Governor Neve for the founding of the town of Los Angeles. To this copy is attached the certificate of Sherman Day, U. S. Surveyor General for California, that it is a true and correct copy of the original document on file in his office. This document, as traced, bears date of Mission of San Gobxxel, August 26th, 1788. Other evidence before us fixed the date of the founding of Los Angeles in September, 1781. In an examination for the discovery of this discrepancy, it was found that Governor Neve was succeeded by Governor Fages on the 7th of September, 1782. It was therefore conclusive that the *scholar* who executed this traced copy, not only transformed Gabriel into the uncouth Gobxxel, but changed the date of 1781 into 1788, and that the United States officer, a highly educated gentleman, of experience and of probity, certified that a document with such gross blunders of the tracer, was a true and correct copy.

The quietude which prevailed in the civil, military and ecclesiastical government of California during the first half of a century after the advent of the Franciscan Missionaries into California, and which was not disturbed by the commotion in which the Government of New Spain was, during the latter half of that period involved, began to give way before questions affecting the inhabitants of California which were agitated in the latter part of the third decade of the present century. With the exception of a slight ripple which manifested itself in the Military District of Monterey previous to 1830, no act of insubordination had transpired up to that time. Even the sovereignty of Spain, which was recognized without any attempt from any quarter to dispute its right up to this time, was quietly laid aside by the civil, military and ecclesiastical rulers on the 9th day of April, 1822, and allegiance to the "Kingdom of the Empire of Mexico" was voluntarily and peacefully assumed by the officers and those in authority, who, up to that day, had sworn only by the King of Spain, and this same quietude still continued under the recognized sovereignty of Mexico, without any public disturbance, until the latter part of 1831, when an insurrection broke forth in the town of Los Angeles, which caused the spilling of the first blood shed in civil strife in California. A large number of the people of Los Angeles had, during the year 1831, assumed an attitude of hostility to the Alcalde, who had put under arrest and placed in confinement some of the influential citizens of the place. It was a matter of belief by the people of Los Angeles that what they looked upon as the arbitrary acts of the Alcalde were inspired by the Governor and Military Commandant of the Territory, Don Manuel Victoria, and in the latter part of November, he being on his way from Monterey to the southern part of the Territory, accompanied by a small military escort, they determined to rid themselves not only of their Alcalde, but the country of its Governor. On the morning of the 5th of December, 1831, the people having liberated those who had been imprisoned by the Alcalde, and made a prisoner of the latter, armed themselves and sallied forth to meet and oppose General Victoria. He was met a few miles from town, when a conflict ensued, in which one of his officers, Captain R. Pacheco—the father of ex-Governor Pacheco—and one of the attacking party, Don Jose Maria Abila, of Los Angeles, were killed. The General received a sword wound from Abila before the latter was killed. The combatants separated immediately after these casualties. The General, leaving Los Angeles to his right, repaired to San Gabriel Mission, where on the following day he surrendered up his authority to the insurgents, who sent him to San Diego, from which place he shortly after embarked for the coast of Mexico.

For some time after the expulsion of General Victoria, Los Angeles was the seat of government of those who expelled him. The head of the government was General Jose Maria Echandia, who had been the predecessor of Victoria. His jurisdiction, however, only extended over the southern part of the territory. The people of the northern portion of the territory adhered to the government of General Victoria, and sustained, as the rightful head of the civil and military government of California, Captain Agustin V. Zamorano, the military officer next in rank to the General. This division was not healed until General Figueroa reached California in 1833.

The Congress of Mexico erected the town of Los Angeles into a city in 1836, and shortly after appointed Carlos Antonio Carrillo, of Santa Barbara, the civil Governor of California. Upon receiving the appointment of Governor, the seat of government was established by Governor Carrillo in Los Angeles, August, 1837. His authority, as Governor, was not recognized by the people north of Santa Barbara, and after a few months he succumbed to Governor Juan B. Alvarado, who had been acting as Governor from the 6th of November, 1836.

After the adoption by Mexico of the centralized form of government, and the transformation, under that government, of the States and Territories into Departments, and the subdivision of the latter into Prefectures, Los Angeles City was the seat of the Prefecture of the Southern District of California, from some time in 1839 to about the close of 1843, when that system of government was abandoned. Tiburcio Tapia, a native of Los Angeles, was the first Prefect, and held the office about one year, when he was succeeded by Santiago Arguello, who continued in office until July, 1843, when Manuel Dominguez was appointed, and held the office until December of that year. Mr. Dominguez was a member of the convention that framed the State Constitution, and still lives upon his San Pedro Ranch.

In the Summer of 1835, a small body of men, natives of Sonora and other Mexican States, having as leaders one Torres and Apalatey, collected at the Los Nietos Ranch and marched into the Town of Los Angeles, for the professed object of overthrowing the government of Figueroa and placing Mr. Ijar at the head of affairs. They took and held the town a few hours, when they betrayed their leaders, delivering them up to the regular authorities, and then dispersed.

Some time in 1835, the paramour of a married woman, abeted by the wife, murdered the husband while on his way from Los Angeles City to his residence. The parties to the homicide were soon arrested and lodged in prison. At that time there was no Court, or civil authority in California, which was invested with power to execute the sentence of death. In cases in which the punishment was death, the record of the trial was required to be sent to Mexico for inspection and approval by superior criminal officers, before the sentence could be executed. As this was attended with great delay, and the means of keeping prisoners under sentence were inadequate for their secure detention, the inhabitants of Los Angeles, after the trial had taken place and their guilt fully established, demanded of the Alcalde the surrender of these two prisoners, that they might be executed without any further delay. Although the demand was not granted no effort was made by the lawful authorities to prevent the execution of the demand. A body of armed men took the two prisoners from their place of confinement, and they were both publicly shot.

In April, 1838, a small body of men, under the command of Clemente Espinosa, an ensign, was sent from Santa Barbara by Colonel Jose Maria Villa, a partizan of Governor Alvarado and General Castro, to capture certain persons suspected of being engaged in a plan to overthrow the government of Alvarado, and replace Governor Carrillo in authority. The party of Espinosa entered Los Angeles in the night, and camped on the open space in front of the old Catholic Church. The inhabitants discovered upon opening the doors of their dwellings on the following morning that the town had been captured, or rather that it was then held by armed men from abroad, who soon commenced a general search in the houses of the citizens for the suspected persons. Quite a number were arrested, among whom were Jose Antonio Carrillo, a brother of the deposed Governor, Pio Pico, Andres Pico and Gil Ybarra, the then Alcalde of Los Angeles, together with about half a dozen more of the most prominent native citizens of the place. They were all taken north as prisoners of war. The only casualty which occurred was the breaking of the arm of J. J. Warner, by one of Espinosa's men, in consequence of his inability to inform them where Don Pio Pico could be found, and his resistance to an order of arrest for refusing permission to have his house searched for suspected persons.

In November, 1842, Commodore Thomas ap Catesby Jones, with his official suite of the United States navy, paid an official and apologetical visit to General Manuel Micheltorena, at Los Angeles. This interview grew out of the capture of Monterey, the Capital of California, by Commodore Jones on the 20th of the preceding month.

A bloodless battle, of two or three days' continuance, was fought in the San Fernando valley in the month of February, 1845, between Governor Micheltorena, at the head of the troops which accompanied him to California from Mexico, and General Jose Castro, at the head of citizens and residents of the southern part of California, who had been hastily collected and armed to meet and oppose Micheltorena, who was marching upon Los Angeles from Monterey. The result of the battle was the surrender of Micheltorena and his expulsion from California.

Upon the expulsion of Micheltorena Los Angeles again became the seat of government, with Don Pio Pico as Governor, whose authority was recognized throughout California until the occupation of the country by the Americans, in 1846.

On the 7th of August, 1846, the American squadron, under Commodore R. F. Stockton, anchored in the bay of San Pedro. Col. J. C. Fremont, at the head of his command of volunteers, which had occupied San Diego in the latter part of the preceding month, was then approaching Los Angeles from San Diego. Commodore Stockton, upon anchoring at San Pedro, landed four hundred men and some artillery. Having formed a junction with the force under Fremont, he moved upon, and on the 15th of August occupied Los Angeles City. Governor Pico and General Castro abandoned the city a short time before its occupation by Commodore Stockton. The Governor made his way, without discovery by the American forces, through San Diego into Lower California, and thence crossed the Gulf and landed in Sonora. General Castro, after disbanding the force under his command, took the road, with a small number of adherents, for Sonora, over the Colorado River route. Some little effort was made by the Americans to capture both him and Governor Pico, but they made good their escape.

On the 23d of the following September, (Commodore Stockton and Colonel Fremont, having some time previous left Los Angeles for San Francisco), the quarters of the Americans under A. H. Gillespie, a Lieutenant of Marines, who had been left by Stockton as Military Commandant at Los Angeles, were attacked by Cervol Varelas, a native of Los Angeles, at the head of a few of his countrymen. Three days thereafter the Hon. B. D. Wilson, who had been placed in command of a few men at the Jarupa Ranch, to protect the inhabitants of that section of country and their property from Indian raids, and who had been ordered by Gillespie to come to his relief, was captured, together with his small command, at the Chino Ranch, to which place he had repaired upon discovering that the march of his small body of men was being threatened by the forces of Varelas and Diego Sepulveda. In the meantime, and until the 30th of September, the siege of Gillespie was continued, and seeing no way of raising the siege, after learning of the capture of Wilson's party, he signed articles of capitulation on the 30th, and marching the garrison to San Pedro, embarked it on board an American merchant ship lying there at anchor.

On the 6th of October, Captain Mervin, in the frigate Savannah, anchored at San Pedro. On the, following day he debarked, as also did the force under Gillespie, and at the head of his marines and the men under Gillespie took up his march for Los Angeles. His force amounted in all to five hundred men. The insurgents at Los Angeles were not inactive during this time. A force, with one small piece of artillery, was organized under Jose Antonio Carrillo and Jose Maria Flores, and sent to check the approach of Captain Mervin. Some slight skirmishing was done along the line of march during the 7th, but on the 8th, after a spirited engagement which lasted for an hour or more, Captain Mervin, who up to this time continued his advance, becoming alarmed at the resistance which he encountered, and the loss of men he was suffering, ordered a retreat, and reaching the shore of San Pedro, immediately embarked his forces.

On the 1st of November Commodore Stockton, who had returned to San Pedro, landed eight hundred men, for the purpose of marching upon and capturing Los Angeles. Instead, however, of taking up the line of march for Los Angeles he re-embarked his forces, and, with the squadron, sailed for San Diego.

On the 8th of January, 1847, Commodore Stockton having been joined at San Diego by General Kearny and his escort of dragoons, with which he had arrived at that place from New Mexico, reached the San Gabriel River in his march upon Los Angeles from San Diego. The insurgents, under the command of Jose Maria Flores, who had attained to the rank of General-in-Chief, occupying the right bank of the river, opposed the crossing, but it was effected without much loss on the part of the Americans, and with but little on the part of the Californians. On the following day the American column, while on the march, was attacked by the forces of Flores. This attack took place between the Laguna and the Mesa, some four or five miles southeasterly from Los Angeles City, and is sometimes called the battle of the Laguna, and sometimes that of the Mesa. On the following day, January 10th, Commodore Stockton and General Kearney entered the City of Los Angeles.

The insurgent force, under Flores, failing to make any impression upon the Americans in their attack upon the marching column on the 9th, was moved to San Pasqual, some five or six miles northeast of Los Angeles. On the night of the 11th, at an early hour, General Flores, with forty or fifty men, started for Sonora, going by the way of the San Gorgonio Pass and the Colorado River.

Colonel Fremont had with him when he reached San Fernando, on the 11th of January, Jose Jesus Pico, a native Californian, a resident of San Luis Obispo, a man of some prominence among his fellow countrymen, and who had been captured as a spy and brought into San Luis Obispo by Colonel Fremont's command, where he was tried and sentenced, by a court-martial, to be executed. The sentence was, however, remitted by Colonel Fremont, and from that time onward Mr. Pico ever manifested a sincere desire to advance the interests of Colonel Fremont.

The day after Commodore Stockton left San Diego, on his march upon Los Angeles, he sent a bearer of dispatches to Colonel Fremont, informing him of his departure, accompanied by General Kearney, from San Diego for Los Angeles. The bearer of these dispatches left San Diego by water, and landing at San Buenaventura, overtook Fremont and delivered to him Commodore Stockton's dispatches before he entered San Fernando.

On the night of the 11th, at about midnight, Jose Jesus Pico came into the camp of the Californians, at San Pasqual, and gave them the information that Colonel Fremont had reached San Fernando, and he urged their leaders to open communications and enter into negotiations with Colonel Fremont, instead of attempting to negotiate with Commodore Stockton.

General Andres Pico, who succeeded to the command upon the departure of Flores, instructed Francisco Rico and Francisco de la Guerra to accompany Jose Jesus Pico on his return to San Fernando that same night, and to have an interview with Colonel Fremont and learn from him his views respecting negotiations. After having met Colonel Fremont at San Fernando, Messrs. Rico and De la Guerra returned to San Pasqual early in the morning of the 12th. Immediately after their return to the camp, Don Jose Antonio Carrillo and Don Agustin Olvera were appointed and commissioned by General Pico, to meet and negotiate terms of capitulation with commissioners to be appointed by Colonel Fremont. General Pico immediately broke up his camp at San Pasqual, and with his entire command accompanied his commissioners to Providencia. Colonel Fremont with his command, also left San Fernando on the morning of the 12th, and marched to Cahuenga, some four or five miles from Providencia. An interview took place between Colonel Fremont and some two or three of the leading men of General Pico's party, on the road, about midway between San Fernando and Cahuenga. The commissioners which had been named by General Pico met the commissioners appointed by Colonel Fremont, at Cahuenga, soon after the arrival of Colonel Fremont at the latter place, when the treaty was drawn up and signed by the commissioners, and was then ratified by General Pico and Colonel Fremont, and exchanged on the 13th.

It can hardly be presumed that Colonel Fremont, was ignorant at the time he entered into negotiations with the Californians, that Commodore Stockton and General Kearny had taken possession of Los Angeles, and that he could have opened communications with them had he been so inclined.

Commodore Stockton, while on the march upon Los Angeles from San Diego, had been met at San Juan Capistrano by William Workman and Charles Fluggee, the first a native of England, the second of Germany, both old and prominent residents of Los Angeles, who had been sent by General Flores to obtain from Commodore Stockton the terms upon which he would receive the submission of the insurgent forces. They were told by Commodore Stockton, that he would guarrantee the lives and property of all others who had taken part in the insurrection, only upon the unconditional surrender to him of the person of General Flores. To these terms neither the commissioners or any of the Californians were prepared to accede.

It is apparent that the Californians had good cause to urge them into negotiations with Colonel Fremont, or any other person who could guarantee them more honorable terms than the unconditional surrender of their commanding officer. But the motive which induced Colonel Fremont to seek for the Californians, and open negotiations with them, instead of attempting to open communications with Stockton and Kearny, must be left to conjecture.

During the time of the insurrection there had been an extra session of the Mexican Territorial Legislature, at Los Angeles City. Commodore Stockton knowing this fact, and wishing to open communications with some person, or some recognized body that had exercised executive or legislative authority during the insurrection, and unable to find any executive or military officer with whom to treat, did, on the second day after his entrance into the city, send safe conducts to such of the members of the legislative body as he could learn were in the neighborhood, and invited them to repair to Los Angeles and enter into negotiations. He did not meet with success in this attempt. The whereabouts of some of the members could not be found and others declined the invitation.

The arrival of General Fremont on the 14th, and the promulgation of the fact that he had made a treaty with General Pico, caused considerable discussion between Stockton, Kearny and Fremont. Neither Stockton or Kearny was disposed to recognize the treaty made by Fremont as binding on them. Matters continued in an unsatisfactory condition until the 16th, when an additional article having been added to the treaty by the commissioners, and ratified by Colonel Fremont and General Pico, who, in the mean time, had come into the city, the treaty was accepted by Commodore Stockton as the basis for the pacification of the country.

The occupation of Los Angeles by the Americans in the month of August, 1846, was, like that of the whole Territory of Upper California in that and the preceeding month, accomplished without bloodshed or the firing of a gun. The discontent, which was manifested by the inhabitants of Spanish ancestry, and which, in September, culminated in an insurrection which regained possession of all that part of California south and east of Monterey, was caused by the ill-advised acts of some of the American officers left in charge of the little garrisons stationed at the principal centres of population.

In Los Angeles, the officer in command, Lieutenant Gillespie, of the Marine Corps, with numerically an insignificant and undisciplined military force, attempted by a coercive system to effect a moral and social change in the habits, diversions and pastimes of the people, and reduce them to his standard of propriety. The result of this injudicious effort was the rebellion of the inhabitants. The revolt inaugurated in this city immediately spread throughout the country as far north as Monterey.

There was but little or no intercourse between the people of California and those of other nations, or even with those of other parts of New Spain, for the first fifty years after the planting of the missions. Although the missionaries and the military officers were in correspondence with their superiors at the cities of Mexico and Chihuahua, this correspondence was not only infrequent but irregular, and was chiefly transmitted by vessels between San Blas and California, the passages of which occupied a long time and were far apart.

Between 1820 and 1825 foreign vessels began to call at and to trade in the ports of California. Most of these foreign vessels were American, but they gave to the world but little knowledge of California.

After the Independence of Mexico, and the opening of its ports to foreign trade, the port of San Pedro was one of the chief points on the Coast of California for the shipping of the products of the country, and for the landing of goods, wares and merchandise from abroad. The three missions in this county, and the owners of stock-farms, and the inhabitants of Los Angeles disposed of their products, chiefly hides and tallow, on board of foreign merchant vessels at the anchorage of San Pedro, taking imported products and manufactures in payment.

Between the people of Sonora, or of New Mexico, and those of California, there was comparatively no intercourse until about 1830. The intercourse between those places and California, which commenced about that time, was mainly brought about through the enterprise of American trappers or beaver hunters.

Jedediah S. Smith, of the Rocky Mountain Fur Company, and a leader of trapping parties, came into California with a party of trappers from the Yellowstone River in 1825, and again in 1826. Through him and his men, others engaged in trapping beaver in the Rocky Mountains, learned something of California. In 1828-9 Ewing Young, of Tennessee, who had for some seasons been engaged in trapping beaver in and north of New Mexico, made a hunt in the Tulare Valley and on the waters of the San Joaquin. He had in his party some natives of New Mexico. He passed through Los Angeles on his way back from his hunting fields to New Mexico. His men, on their return to New Mexico, in the Summer of 1830, spread their reports of California over the northern part of that Territory. In 1830 William Wolfskill, a native of Kentucky but from Missouri, fitted out, in conjunction with Mr. Young, a trapping party at Taos, New Mexico, to hunt the waters of the San Joaquin and Sacramento Valleys. Failing, in the winter of 1830-31, to get over the mountains between Virgin River and those rivers discharging into the Bay of San Francisco, and his men becoming demoralized and impatient from their sufferings of cold, he changed his line of travel and came with his party into Los Angeles in February, 1831. With Mr. Wolfskill's party there were a number of New Mexicans, some of whom had taken *serapes* and *fresadas* (woolen blankets) with them for the purpose of trading them to the Indians in exchange for beaver skins. On their arrival in California they advantageously disposed of their blankets to the rancheros in exchange for mules. These New Mexicans mostly returned to Santa Fe in the summer of 1831, with the mules they had obtained in California. The appearance of these mules in New Mexico, owing to their large size, compared with those at that time used in the Missouri and Santa Fe trade, and their very fine form, as well as the price at which they had been bought in barter for blankets, caused quite a sensation in New Mexico, out of which sprang up a trade, carried on by means of caravans or pack animals, between the two sections of the same country which flourished for some ten or twelve years. These caravans reached California yearly during the before mentioned time. They brought the woolen fabrics of New Mexico, and carried back mules, and silk, and other Chinese goods.

Los Angeles was the central point in California of this New Mexican trade. Coming by the northern or Green and Virgin River routes, the caravans came through the Cajon Pass and reached Los Angeles. From thence they scattered themselves over the country from San Diego to San Jose, and across the Bay to Sonoma and San Rafael. Having bartered and disposed of the goods brought, and procured such as they wished to carry back, and what mules they could drive, they concentrated at Los Angeles for their yearly return.

Between 1831 and 1844 a considerable number of native New Mexicans and some foreign residents of that Territory, came through with the trading caravans, in search of homes in this country. Some of them became permanent citizens, or residents, of this county. Julian Chaves, of this city, and who has served many terms as County Supervisor or Common Councilman of the city, was among the first immigrants. The Martinezes, of San Jose, and the Trujillos, and others, were also among these immigrants. Of foreigners, who were residents of New Mexico, and came during this period and located in this county, were John Rowland, William Workman, John Reed, all of whom are dead, and the Hon. B. D. Wilson, and David W. Alexander, heretofore and now the Sheriff of this county. Doctor John Marsh also came to California in company with these traders, and after residing in Los Angeles some years, he located near Mount Diablo, where he continued to live until he was murdered.

Other parties of Americans found their way from New Mexico to California at different times in the third and fourth decades of this century, numbers of whom became permanent residents of Los Angeles.

Richard Laughlin and Nathaniel Pryor, both of whom died in Los Angeles, and Jesse Ferguson, who lived here many years, came from New Mexico, by the way of the Gila River, in 1828. In 1831 a Mr. Jackson who had been one of the firm of the Rocky Mountain Fur Company, and a partner of Jedediah S. Smith, came to Los Angeles from Santa Fe for the purpose of buying mules for the Louisiana market. He returned to New Mexico with the mules he purchased. With him came J. J. Warner, who remained in this place. A Mr. Bowman, known here as Joaquin Bowman, was one of J. S. Smith's men, He died at San Gabriel, after having been the miller at the Mission Mill for many years.

In the winter of 1832-3 a small party of Americans from New Mexico came over the Gila River route into Los Angeles. In this small party came Joseph Paulding, who, in 1833 and 1834, made the first two billiard tables of mahogony wood made in California. The first was made for George Rice, and the second for John Rhea, both Americans. Mr. Rice came to California about 1827, from the Sandwich Islands. Mr. Rhea was from North Carolina, and came with Mr. Wolfskill. Lemuel Carpenter, of Missouri, was also of this party, and established a soap manufactory on the right bank of the San Gabriel River, not far from the present road to Los Nietos. Subsequently he became the proprietor of the Santa Gertrudes Ranch, where he died. Wm. Chard was also of this party. After residing in this city some years and planting a vineyard, he removed to the Sacramento Valley. A Mr. Sill, who also settled in the Sacramento Valley, was of this party.

. Ewing Young came into Los Angeles from New Mexico, in March, 1832, with a trapping party of about thirty men. On this occasion he came down the Gila River. With him in this party came a number of men who took up their residence in California; of which number Isaac Williams was a prominent citizen of Los Angeles City for about ten years, when he established himself at the Chino Ranch as a farmer and stock-breeder, and was the proprietor of and resident upon that ranch at the time of the capture there of B. D. Wilson and party, as heretofore related. He continued to reside there until his death in September, 1856. Moses Carson, a brother of the renowned Kit Carson, came with Young at this time. After residing here a number of years, he removed to Russian River in this State.

The town of Los Angeles, from its settlement onward, for more than fifty years, had a population greater than any other of the towns of California. The first census, of which there are any records, was taken in 1836, and the sum total of inhabitants of the city and country, over which the authorities of the city exercised jurisdiction, which country included the whole of the present County of Los Angeles, except San Juan Capistrano, which at that time was attached to the district of San Diego, was two thousand two hundred and twenty-eight. Of this number five hundred and fifty-three were domesticated Indians.

This census gives the number of forty-six of the residents of Los Angeles as foreigners, and of these twenty-one are classed as Americans.

Knowing that the following letters were in the archives of the Society of California Pioneers, and desirous that the evidence of the discovery and working of gold placeres in this county might be incorporated into this sketch, a request was made to the Secretary of that Society for copies of the letters. Owing to unavoidable delay in their arrival, we were under the necessity of preparing that part of this sketch from the personal recollection of one of the writers, and such other evidence as could be obtained from witnesses still living.

After the preceding pages were printed, copies of the letters were received. A discrepancy in the date of the discovery as related by Mr. Stearns and that given in these pages will be observed. We believe, however, that the date given by us is the correct one, as, among the many authorities for that date is Don Ygnacio del Valle of Camuloa, an intelligent and educated gentleman, a man of careful habits, and whose practice has been to make and preserve notes of the events of his life. In the year of the discovery of these gold fields Mr. Valle was appointed an auxiliary Alcalde, expressly for that mining district, and is less likely to be mistaken than Mr. Stearns when writing upon the subject after a lapse of twenty-five years, and who being a merchant at that time, would upon referring to his books, be more likely to find the date of the purchase of the gold, than that of the discovery of the gold fields.

The letters are given in full, as the one from Mr. Robinson vividly portrays the secluded state of California at that time.

Los Angeles, July 8th, 1867.

Louis R. Lull, Esq., Secretary of the Society of Pioneers, San Francisco.

Sir:—On my arrival here from San Francisco, some days since, I received your letter of June 3d last past, requesting the certificate of assay of gold sent by me to the Mint at Philadelphia in 1842. I find by referring to my old account books that November 22d, 1842, I sent by Alfred Robinson, Esq., (who returned from California to the States by the way of Mexico,) twenty ounces California weight (18¾ ounces Mint weight) of placer gold, to be forwarded by him to the U. S. Mint at Philadelphia for assay.

In his letter to me, dated August 6th, 1843, you will find a copy from the Mint assay of the gold, which letter I herewith enclose to you to be placed in the archives of the Society.

The placer mines from which this gold was taken were first discovered by Francisco Lopez, a native of California, in the month of March, 1842, at a place called San Francisquito, about thirty-five miles north-west from this city (Los Angeles.)

The circumstances of the discovery by Lopez, as related by him, are as follows: Lopez, with a companion, was out in search of some stray horses, and about midday they stopped under some trees and tied their horses out to feed, they resting under the shade; when Lopez with his sheath knife dug up some wild onions, and in the dirt discovered a piece of gold, and searching further found some more. He brought these to town, and showed them to his friends, who at once declared there must be a placer of gold. This news being circulated, numbers of the citizens went to the place and commenced prospecting in the neighborhood, and found it to be a fact that there was a placer of gold. After being satisfied most persons returned; some remained, particularly Sonorenses (Sonorians), who were accustomed to work in placers. They met with good success.

From this time the placers were worked with more or less success, and principally by Sonorenses (Sonorians), until the latter part of 1846, when most of the Sonorenses left with Captain Flores for Sonora.

While worked there was some six or eight thousand dollars taken out per annum.

Very respectfully, yours,
ABEL STEARNS.

NEW YORK, August 6th, 1843.

My Dear D. Abel:—I embrace this opportunity of the sailing of a ship from Boston to address you a few lines, and therein to inform you of the result of your shipment of gold, which is as follows, as per statement from the Mint at Philadelphia:

"Memorandum of gold bullion deposited the 8th day of July, 1843, at the mint of the United States at Philadelphia, by Grant & Stone, of weight and value as follows:

"Before melting, 18 34-100 oz.; after melting, 18 1-100 oz.; fineness, 926-1,000; value, $344 75; deduct expenses, sending to Philadelphia and agency there, $4 02; net, $340 73.

I called upon your brother immediately on my arrival here, and stated to him that I should be prepared to deliver him, on your account, $200, as soon as I had disposed of some gold I had in my possession, belonging to you, and accordingly as soon as realized, I paid over the amount, for which I have a receipt. I have making, and intend to send by this conveyance, the boots you ordered, and the remainder you will receive by a vessel which we contemplate sending this fall. Perhaps I may send the jewelry for Dona Arcadia, but the clothing I must defer, as my wife cannot at present attend to the purchasing of it, being rather unwell.

How pleased you would be to make a visit to your native country—your home! What a change you would find—what improvements!

You will be enabled to come via Panama, or rather, I should say, per Canal. The Messrs. Baring & Co., of London, have made a contract with the "Central Government," and in all probability the contract will be finished in five years; so at last the long talked of route through the isthmus will finally be accomplished.

Mexico is still in an unsettled state, and Santa Ana is, to all intents and purposes, Dictator. All and everything is done that he orders, and, in fact, his will is law. I did not see him when I was there, he being so ill-humored that he refused to see any one. The foreign Ministers all had been trying for several days to get at him, but to no purpose. The cause of his wish to be alone was the chagrin he felt at his unsuccessful attempt to subdue the Yucatanos.

Texas still holds out, and there is a rumor of a negotiation under way between Santa Ana and Houston, relative to a peace between the two countries.

In Spain there is another revolution against the Regent. Espartero has met with great reverses. This country seems doomed to civil discord and strife.

Ireland, also, is in agitation, and England has been pouring in troops by thousands through fear of 'n revolt.

The Liberals of England have had sympathetic meetings in favor of the repealers. They seem to think that by placing the Irish on an equality with the English, by giving them equal rights, the Irish will be satisfied. O'Connell, by his harangues, is working them up to a determination; and Ireland shall be a Nation.

You will see by the papers that we have had a change in the Cabinet at Washington. Webster retired and Lagare died.

I informed your brother of this opportunity to write, and he said that he was going a journey—that, if he got back in time, he would make you up a bundle.

Remember me kindly to your wife, to Isadora, Don. Juan and lady, and to all our numerous friends in Los Angeles, and believe me, your friend,

ROBINSON.

I send you six pairs of boots, each $4 50—$27—which have been made from the best of stock.

CHAPTER II.

THE YEAR 1847 hails the dawn of a New Era for California. At the close of January, the authority of the United States was established throughout this territory. The principal incidents of the reoccupation of the City of Los Angeles are related in the unpublished Journal of Dr. John S. Griffin, Assistant Surgeon, U. S. A., attached to the command of General Stephen W. Kearny.

Commodore Stockton and General Kearny took up the line of march from San Diego on the 29th day of December, 1846. The brave little army of six hundred men, was composed of crews of the frigate Congress and sloops of war Portsmouth and Cyane, Company C, First Dragoons of Gen. Kearny, and volunteers, together with thirty native Californians, who were under Captain Santiago E. Arguello. January seventh they encamped at the Rancho of Los Coyotes, about eighteen miles from Los Angeles. For the sequel, we follow the Journal:

January 8th.—We left camp early. It was reported that the enemy would certainly give us a brush, as he had crossed the River San Gabriel in force, with three pieces of artillery. His scouts were hovering around all day. About two and a half P. M. we arrived at an Indian village near the River San Gabriel. There were more scouts. We formed in line of battle. The volunteer riflemen led as scouts; then the dragoons, Cyane's musketeers, four pieces of artillery, marines and sailors; baggage in the centre; cattle and rear guard, with two pieces of artillery. Proceeding thus, the enemy appeared in full force. A hundred or more crossed, threatening our advance, but soon retired and took post on the opposite side. Their grape fell short. Steadily we advanced—the dragoons and Cyane's marines supporting two guns in front; two large guns followed, supported by marines and crew of the Congress. In this shape we took the river, ran off the enemy, and made a lodgment under the first bank.

Our shots here dismounted one or two of their guns—one of these effective shots was aimed and fired by the Commodore. At once we made a rush for the second bank, over a plain of nearly three hundred yards (as I judged) in breadth, between the two points. Across this the charge was made under full fire. When about half way, a charge was threatened; the sailors threw themselves into square, and, with the greatest ease, drove off the enemy. Our charge pressed on and gained the height, many of our men not firing a gun. The Mexicans ran clearly off the field. We had one man killed, eight wounded in the fight, and another by the accidental discharge of a musket. We lost twenty-one horses, of the volunteers, which they had tied up before going into action, and forgot until too late.

9th.—At leaving camp we saw few of the enemy, although he had encamped within a mile the evening before. Proceeding, he appeared in considerable force on our right flank. The artillery exchanged shots. What damage we did I do not know; on our side, a dragoon (Childs) and a sailor were slightly wounded, and Captains Gillespie and Rowan, of the navy, were hit by spent balls. For two miles over this *mesa*, the Mexican artillery fire continued. We were obliged to march slow, in consequence of the broken down condition of the ox teams; nor could we leave the baggage to charge their guns, which we could have easily captured. At length the enemy drew up in open order, at some distance out of gun shot, threatening our right rear and left front. Finally they charged, received an effective fire in return, withdrew, and marched in the direction of the town.

We encamped on the stream, two miles below the city, in which everything was quiet through the night. Occasionally a light could be seen passing about, but no demonstration against us was made.

10th.—About nine o'clock A. M., a flag of truce came out, with information that our entry would not be opposed, since they did not wish the place to be destroyed. We however marched up in line of battle, prepared for action.

The army passed from the river into Main street near the old "Celis house," thence up Main street to the Plaza. Two guns with a couple of hundred men, were stationed on the hill overlooking Main street; the rest quartered as comfortably as possible. On the 14th, Colonel J. C. Fremont marched in from Cahuenga, his battalion, the Journal says, "a body of fine-looking men in general on good horses and armed with rifles." Eleven hundred of United States troops were now in the city. Upon the hill at once was commenced a Fort, on which the patriotic sailors worked cheerily, although they had begun to talk of their ships, and the term of service of many of them had expired. It was finished by the Mormons. It has been said that a small entrenchment at this spot existed, made in the time of Governor Micheltorena. This is a mistake. Before 1846 it had been the play-ground of the children, favorite resort of lovers, the place for picnics or recreation on days of festival. In 1850 and several years thereafter, hundreds of persons every fine Sunday afternoon of early Spring, might be seen there, culling the wild flowers or gazing over the beautiful panorama of mountain and plain and sea. A very long time passed before it began to have charming residences as now. January eighteenth, General Kearny, with his dragoons afoot and almost shoeless, and after the casualties of their hard campaign, scarcely more than fifty in number, marched for San Diego. Captains Emory and Turner, Lieutenants Davidson and Warner, and Dr. Griffin, returned with him. Commodore Stockton followed the next day.

The battle-ground of January eighth, is at present "Pico Crossing;" by the Californians always named CURUNGA. General Jose Maria Flores commanded the Californians. He had ordered the charge to be made by a squadron. The company advanced, under Captain Juan Bautista Moreno. Don Francisco Cota, bearing the Mexican standard, placed himself at its head, and the column dashed down the precipitous hill, about seventy in number, upon the close ranks of Stockton. The sailors received them with a terrible fire. The other company reached the brow of the hill to follow their comrades; when Don Diego Sepulveda, acting upon his own judgment, ordered a halt, advanced alone, and commanded a retreat. He was aid of Flores. This feat was accomplished by Captain Moreno, under heavy fire, but without further loss than a severe wound which he received. Two had been mortally wounded by the first fire of the sailors; namely, Ygnacio Sepulveda ('El Cuacho'), brother of Don Diego, and Francisco Rubiou ('Bachico'). They died of their wounds, at San Gabriel. Californians still speak of their strange emotions, retired only about a thousand yards, at the music of Stockton's Band, when the heights were taken and their late camp occupied by him. In the artillery duel of the MESA, Alferez Jose Maria Ramirez was slightly wounded, and a youth named Ignacio 'El Guaimeno,' killed. Their entire force did not exceed four hundred. Solely on a point of honor, they say, were made the demonstrations of this second day, not from any serious plan or design to give battle. At the distance, it was easy for the American army to be misled as to the effect of its shots, owing to the habit of Californians, so agile on horseback, to hang themselves on their saddles over their horses, on either side from the danger. 'El Guaimeno,' that is to say, 'of Guaimas,' was a Yaqui Indian, born on the river of that name. In a battle against the Yaquis, a soldier had captured him, then a child, and was about to kill him. Don Santiago Johnson interposed, bought him of the soldier for twelve dollars, and finally brought him in his family to California.

This account of the engagements, except as to the origin of 'El Guaimeno,' is derived from Don Agustin Olvera, who was present as "Capitan Auxiliar," and also as a member of the Departmental Assembly. It seems to have been thought, that the personal eclat of some of the higher functionaries would inspire the rank and file with greater enthusiasm. Certainly common sense will not undertake to judge them, as regular soldiers. Magnificent horsemen they were, and by a simple and active life, made hardy for campaigns, but never had rigid military training. Most of them were very young. This *revolucion* owed much to the patriotic zeal of the women of the country, by fervent appeal and indignant upbraiding impelling father, brother, husband, lover, to resistance. Happily they the first in January to bow gracefully to destiny—a gentle influence so new-born, like the rainbow at the close of the storm. Many of the graver inhabitants felt that they were not able to cope with the United States; their men undisciplined, and without any resources to wage war. So thought General Flores, we may well believe, with his reputation for experience and skill; and the like conviction has often been attributed to General Andres Pico. But the untamed spirit of the majority at first did not stop to reason upon the consequences. Honor and love of country threw away cold calculation and military caution.

General Jose Maria Flores was born at the Hacienda de los Ornos, in the department of Coahuila. He had been aid to Governor Micheltorena. He died at Mazatlan, in April or May, 1866. His wife was a native of California—Dona Dolores Zamorano, daughter of Don Agustin Zamorano, who had been Secretary of Governor Jose Maria Echeandia from 1825, and afterward, in 1833, of Governor Jose Figueroa; he was born in Florida. Her grandfather was Don Santiago Arguello, formerly Military Commandant at San Diego, and from 1840 until 1843, Prefect at Los Angeles, whose eldest son, Don Santiago E., was captain of the native Californian company, on the American side, at the battle of Curunga. General Flores was thirty years of age, at the date of these events.

From September, 1846, this city was the centre of exciting operations. Late in October, Don Leonardo Cota, at the head of one hundred men, raised in and around Los Angeles, marched for San Diego, of which port Commodore Stockton, in the frigate Congress, a short time before had taken possession. After an unimportant demonstration on the Old Presidio hill, and a trifling skirmish at the Mission San Diego, he withdrew to the little valley of Soledad, twelve miles north of the town, near enough to avail himself of any opportunity that might offer to renew the attack. His officers were Enrique Abila, Ramon Carrillo, Jose Maria Cota, Carlos Dominguez, Nicolas Hermosillo (a Sonoranian), all of this city; Jose Alipaz of San Juan Capistrano, and Ramon O. Suna of San Diego. Meanwhile a Commission that had been sent by Flores to Castro, in Sonora, had despatched information to Los Angeles, that a large body of armed men had been seen on the river Gila. In consequence of this report, about November twenty-second, General Andres Pico was sent, with one hundred men, to protect Cota and oppose the entry of any hostile force. General Pico first took post at San Luis Rey Mission; finally moved to the pretty valley of San Pascual. He then had eighty men; having lost some stragglers, but gained reinforcements of ten from San Diego county, among them Don Leandro Osuna. His officers were Captain Juan Bautista Moreno, Tomas A. Sanchez, Pablo Vejar, Manuel Vejar, and others. The reader will not confound this point with the Rancho of San Pascual, about twelve miles from the City of Los Angeles, where subsequently, about the date of the Cahuenga negotiation, General Pico had a camp. San Pascual of battle memory is thirty-four miles northeast from the City of San Diego, close to the foot of the mountains. This is one of the three Indian pueblos established after the secularization of the Missions. It had then a small population, originally of emancipated Neophytes of the Mission of San Diego, who have been reduced in numbers during the last thirty years. It exists still, but misses the governing hand of "Old Panto," who died two or three years ago.

The fight of DECEMBER SIXTH was due to the impetuosity of General Kearny. General Pico was ill-prepared for it on that night. Warned by Indian runners, coming into his camp, of forces marching from Santa Maria Rancho, yet his horses had been left grazing loose, up San Pascual Valley, until very near the moment of attack. The Californian account gives a loss of two prisoners—one of whom was wounded—none killed. The prisoners were Don Pablo Vejar, and the wounded man, Juan Lara, whose leg, six months afterward, was amputated at San Diego by a French physician, and who for a long time continued to live at Los Angeles. Don Leandro Osuna killed Captain Moore with a lance. In the last fierce onslaught, particularly conspicuous were Juan Lobo, a ranchero of Mision Vieja, Dolores Higuera, commonly called "El Guero," and son of Salvador Higuera—these were privates—and Captain Moreno. Pablo Apis, Indian Chief of Temecula, was not there, nor any other Indians. The scence of conflict being at the Rancheria of Panto, Chief of San Pascual, he had rendered some aid to General Pico. The first shots were fired close to his house—within three hundred yards of which fell Captain Johnston, in the first charge. It is admitted that Phillip Crosthwaite, a San Diego volunteer under Gillespie, saved the life of Don Pablo Vejar, whom one of the two Delaware Indians of Kit Carson was on the point of killing. On the morning after the fight, Don Leonardo Cota incorporated his company with that of General Pico, at the Rancho of San Bernardo, which place, a few hours afterward, was occupied by General Kearny.

After the first shock, at the Indian village, it is evident that the Californians retreated rapidly down the road, except a few who escaped over the hills. Captain Moore and men followed on the second charge, pell mell, one after another, in utter confusion; their fire arms in general useless—from the cold, their sabres almost impotent, and the bugler unable to sound a call. Lieutenant Hammond was heard to say, by William B. Dunne: "For God's sake, men, come up!" In vain, in the manner they were mounted. At the distance of half a mile a sharp, rocky spur makes out from the range of hills. There were a few Americans dead or wounded. Day broke, but with a dense fog. A goodly number, including General Kearny, Captain Moore, Lieutenant Hammond, and Captain Gillespie, had passed by and out into the little plain that spreads beyond toward San Bernardo and Rincon Ranchos. A body of lancers suddenly rushed upon them from behind the north side of this spur. Five minutes completed the massacre. None had been killed or wounded on the way from the Indian village. The howitzer was captured by Guero Higuera and another. He then attacked Captain Gillespie. In 1856, at San Francisco, that officer described to Don Agustin Olvera the incidents of this encounter. He received first a slight wound in the chest, followed up with his sword, and parried other thrusts; at last Higuera's lance struck him full in the mouth with such force as to knock out two teeth. He fell from his horse to the ground, and feigned to be dead. His fine zerape and horse and saddle Higuera seized, and galloped off. When Captain Emory got the other howitzer in place, the men returning from the plain formed in a circle around it, a few Californians still riding near. Presently the fog rose, and they were visible distinctly all making off toward the Soto Hill. Captain Moore was killed, at the distance of several hundred yards on the plain, near a pond of water; his sword hilt was in his hand in death; the blade was found in two pieces. At the point of the spur, above referred to, among the rocks and cactus, the hospital was established; the wounded were brought in from the plain, and the dead were sought for and gathered. In his Report, Captain William H. Emory says: "When night closed in, the bodies were buried under a willow to the east of our camp. Thus were put to rest together, and forever, a band of brave and heroic men. The long march of 2,000 miles had brought our little band to know each other well. Community of hardships, danger, and privations had produced relations of mutual regard which caused their loss to sink deeply into our memories." The saddest reflection of a calm judgment, after the lapse of years, is that, with the character of the Californians, so easily satisfied and so conciliable always, and the known disposition of their commander, General Andres Pico, in the actual circumstances of his country—if General Kearny had marched into the valley of San Pascual, in open daylight and according to military rules, his advent would have been the signal for a treaty of peace and prompt submission to his authority; at any rate, he would have reached San Diego, it is easy to believe from all the circumstances, without the loss of blood on either side.

Three days before the battle of San Pascual, a portion of the men under General Flores, chiefly "Barbarenos" (i. e., of Santa Barbara), rebelling at the proposal to send them to Mexico with certain American prisoners—from an aversion to go out of their native California—rose against him and put him in confinement. The Departmental Assembly met next day, adopted a decree recognizing Flores in supreme command. This was published on the fifth, and tranquility so restored. During these occurrences the white population of this city, is estimated by thoughtful persons then living here, at not over one thousand, which was the estimate of the United States officers when they entered, January, 1847.

A vivid picture of march and battle is presented in Dr. Griffin's Journal:

"1846—November 22.—We discovered the trail of a large body of horse. Kit Carson saw the tracks of women on the sand. Lieutenant Emory went out with a party of twenty men, and about 12½ P. M., brought in three or four Mexicans, from whom we learned that they were a party of traders, or rather refugees from California to Sonora. They had five hundred horses and mules. They told us of Flores; that Roubidoux was a prisoner; advised us not to lose time, as our presence would be of great benefit to our countrymen. (I think, not many minutes will be lost.) * * * Our men are nearly naked and barefooted, their feet sore, and leg-weary. Only the sick have been allowed to ride lately. We are a mile and a half above the mouth of the Gila.

"23d—A child born to night, in the Mexican camp. We all contributed tea, sugar, and coffee to the mother.

"24th.—Lieutenants Emory and Warner (Topographical Engineers), while out making observations, came across a Mexican in the bottom; searched him, and found several letters addressed to Castro. Crossed the Colorado River, so as to take the desert to-morrow.

* * * * * * *

"December 2d.—About 4 P. M. arrived at Warner's—the extreme frontier settlement of California. He is living very comfortably; seems to have plenty of cattle, horses and sheep, and certainly has a fine range for them. An Irishman there informed us * * * that there were detached parties of the enemy between us and San Diego, and that a Mexican force, escorting prisoners out of the country to Mexico, would probably arrive in our neighborhood to-night.

"3d.—This is called Agua Caliente—a boiling spring—a vineyard. We obtained some of the grapes dried; they were nearly as sweet as raisins, and of fine flavor; also, watermelons from the Indians. Last night had a visit from an Englishman, by name Stokes; he has remained neutral during the difficulties. He consented to carry a letter to Commodore Stockton, at San Diego. About one P. M., Lieutenant Davidson returned with some hundred young mules and horses, the major portion utterly worthless to us. * * * Rain all day. Camped at Stokes' Ranch in the evening—Santa Ysabel.

"4th.—This was a Mission; the buildings much better than at Warner's; everything of neater appearance. An Indian village was near the house. The Chief made a speech to the General last evening, in which he declared his wish not to engage in the war in any manner, but that he was perfectly willing to go to work. The General advised him to keep at peace and work hard, and he would be well treated. Stokes seems to have a large stock. His Major-domo gave the officers a supper. He gave the General information of a party of Mexicans at some mission on our road, with 500 animals.

"5th.—Marched from Stokes' Ranch with Senor Bill—William Williams—the Major-domo, for guide. He drank pretty freely the night before; chasing wild horses, presently he was thrown, and said he would go no further. The General had him mounted on a mule, with two of the guard by his side. Bill took us once on the wrong road, but soon corrected the mistake. After a few miles we met Captain Gillespie's party, from San Diego—35 men and one fourpounder. They soon encamped. We marched about 10 miles, to a grove of live oak, with no water, except that which was falling from the heavens. It rained heavily. A party of the enemy being reported in our vicinity, it was first determined that Captain Moore should take sixty men and make a night attack. For some reason the General altered his mind, and sent Lieutenant Hammond, with three men, to reconnoitre. Hammond found the enemy at some ten miles distant, but was discovered. As he galloped off with his party, the Mexicans gave three cheers.

"December 6th—At two P. M. we were all afoot, and expected to surprise the Mexicans. Although we had rain all night our arms were not reloaded; but 'boots and saddles' was the word, and off we went—in search of adventure. Two miles from camp we overtook Gillespie's company, which fell in in the rear. Major Swords was left back with the baggage and thirty men. Another party remained behind with Gillespie's four-pounder. This reduced our fighting men to eighty-five, all told. With these and two howitzers we marched forward.

The morning was excessively cold. We felt it the more, as most of us were wet to the skin. Passing over a mountain, and traveling as near as I can judge ten or eleven miles, we came in sight of the enemy's fires.

"We marched down the mountain. So soon as we arrived on the flat below, the shout and charge commenced from the advance. After running our jaded and broken down mules and horses about three-fourths of a mile the enemy opened fire on us. The balls whistled by awhile, but the light was not sufficient for me to distinguish anything like a line of the enemy; on my left, however, there was a considerable flashing of guns. In a few minutes the enemy broke, and we found that they had made a stand in front of an Indian Rancheria, called San Pascual. Day was just breaking. At this moment a Mexican dashed by; Lieutenant Beale, of the navy, fired several shots, and he fell. Another man galloped by—he had a Mexican look; a dragoon pistol was fired at him without effect, and the dragoon was about to cut him down with a sabre, when I recognized him as one of Gillespie's party. By this time we were much disordered. Some of our men had fast horses, others poor, broken down horses and mules. Captain Moore, however, ordered the charge further; it was made hurly-burly—not more than ten or fifteen men in line, and not forty altogether. On they went. The enemy continued the retreat for about half a mile, when they rallied, and came at us like devils, with their lances. Mounted on swift horses, and most of our firearms having been discharged or missed fire, from the rain of the night before, our advance was at their mercy. Our men wheeled, and a howitzer having been brought up near, rallied on the gun, and drove off the enemy.

"Hammond was the first wounded man I saw. He had been in the advance with Moore, and had a lance wound on the left side, between the eighth and ninth ribs. I told him to go a little further to the rear and I would attend to him. Separated at this moment from him, the General saw me, told ho was wounded, and wished my services. In a few moments Captains Gillespie and Gibson, and others, were found to be wounded. Captain Johnston, who led the first charge, was killed by a gun-shot. I was told he was the only one who received any injury from gun-shot. Moore was killed leading the second charge; and Hammond, it was said (and so he told me), in attempting to rescue Moore. One of Emory's party was killed by the name of Menard; also, one of Gillespie's men; two Sergeants, one Corporal, and eleven privates, of dragoons, and one missing, supposed to be killed. We lost one of our howitzers—the mules were wild and ran off with the piece. Of the three men with it, one was killed, the other two desperately wounded. Upon the whole, we had wounded: four officers, one Sergeant, one Corporal, ten privates, and Mr. Roubidoux, interpreter. Total killed and wounded, thirty-eight. And I should not think there were to exceed fifty men who saw the enemy. We took two prisoners.

"This was an action wherein decidedly more courage than conduct was shown. The first charge was a mistake on the part of Captain Johnston; the second, on the part of Captain Moore.

"We drove the enemy from the field and encamped.

"Dec. 7th.—Marched and took possession of a hill in front of the house of San Bernardo Rancho, after a brief contest for it. The wounded were carried in six ambulances. I sent word to General Pico that I would be most happy to attend to his wounded. He replied that he had none.

"8th.—Made exchange of one prisoner for another. On account of the wounded the General consented to remain. Lieutenant Beale and Kit Carson were sent with despatches to Commodore Stockton. We burnt all the baggage, in order to have as little encumbrance as possible; dismounted the men, and determined to perform the rest of the march on foot. The enemy hovering around, but careful not to come within gun-shot.

"9th.—In camp; nothing going on; the enemy parading about on the hills on the other side of the valley. We are reduced to mule meat.

"10th.—Sergeant Cox died this morning. If reinforcements are not sent we march in the morning, at all hazards. Our animals were grazing quietly at the foot of the hill near camp. At a distance we could see a party of Mexicans driving a band of wild horses toward us. Within half an hour they came on at full speed, intending thus a stampede. Certainly a beautiful sight, as they approached nearer. Waiting awhile, and not coming within gun-shot, our animals were driven out of the way, and by a shout the wild horses was turned—only one mule getting within gun-shot (with a great hide tied to the tail), which was struck, I was told, by forty balls, and finally butchered. A Godsend to us, this being very fat. The General ordered all things to be in readiness for marching in the morning. We all went to bed firmly convinced that we should have to fight our way into San Diego.

"11th.—About two o'clock A. M., the sentinel heard a body of armed men approaching. They were hailed, and, to our great joy, found to be friends sent to our relief from San Diego. They mustered 200 strong—80 marines and 100 sailors. Captain Zielan in charge of the marines, Lieutenant Gray of the whole detachment. Immediately our beds were vacated, and surrendered to our tired comrades. Awaking, at daylight, they found mule soup ready. In turn, they emptied the contents of their haversacks, consisting of jerked beef and bread, and all made a first rate breakfast. The Jack Tars seemed highly delighted with this new role of 'soldiers,' discontented only with the enemy for not having given them a fight before reaching camp. Early in the morning we started for the Rancho of Penasquitos (little stones). The hill sides were well set with wild oats, two or three inches above the surface, green as a wheat field. Collected a hundred head of cattle to-day, in fine condition; and at the ranch picked up a hundred sheep and a barrel of wine (for the sick and wounded). A plentiful supper, and a good night's rest.

"12th.—All arose, freshened with the idea of to-day finishing this long and weary march. Reached San Diego about four P. M. We received the warmest welcome and kindest attention from our naval friends. Everything, so far as it was in the power of the Surgeon of the post, had been prepared for our wounded. The Congress and Portsmouth were at anchor in the bay, and the town was garrisoned by their crews and marines."

Lieutenant Colonel Philip St. George Cooke, and the Mormon battalion, reached the Mission of San Diego, January 29th; Stephen C. Foster, his interpreter. March 17th, with Company C, 1st Dragoons and four companies of his battalion; Col. Cooke took post at this City. The officers of Company C then were: Capt. A. J. Smith, 1st Lieut. J. B. Davidson, 2nd Lieut. George H. Stoneman; the last mentioned officer a graduate of the previous year at West Point. Col. Jonathan D. Stevenson arrived in the latter part of April, with Company G, Capt. Matthew R. Stevenson and Company E, Capt. Nelson Taylor, of the New York Regiment, (Capt. Stevenson is dead. Capt. Taylor was a Brigadier General in the Civil War, and Member of Congress from New York.) May 16th, by order of Col. Cooke, Dr. Griffin was appointed as surgeon at this City, Dr. Sanderson, surgeon of the Mormon battalion, having been ordered to join Gen. Kearny. In June the Mormon battalion was discharged, their term of service being out: one company of which re-enlisted for the war under Capt. Jesse D. Hunter (now resident here), who had commanded Company B of that battalion; Captain Hunter is a native of Kentucky. In August he was appointed Agent for the Indians, who especially in San Diego county had done much damage upon the ranchos.

A pleasant reminiscence there is of Don Juan Abila. Dr. Griffin made his ride within two days and a half from San Diego, in consequence of Col. Cooke's order. At the Alisos rancho his horse was too jaded to proceed. Don Juan immediately gave him—not a bronco, but one of his best saddle horses—with characteristic Californian hospitality. Thus early had confidence and cordial feelings sprung up among this open-hearted race. It is proper to observe, that before the army had felt the amenities of resident foreigners identified by marriage with the natives—among them, Don Edward Stokes, of Santa Ysabel, and Don Juan Forster, both these gentlemen of English birth.

July 4th, 1847, the Fort on the hill was finished. The staff was raised and the flag thrown to the breeze amid salutes of cannon: and this work was christened Fort Moore. A grand ball at night, given by the American officers, ended that National Anniversary.

It is the name of Capt. Ben. Moore, who had fallen at San Pascual, December 6th, 1846. One, on the then western frontier well-remembered, so kind and genial ever; stern, prompt, faithful when duty called. On that dark day near by fell Lieut. Thomas H. Hammond. Companions they in arms, married to sisters, devoted friends, their life-blood mingled for their country's sake. They are buried together at the Old Town, San Diego.

July 9th, Lieut. Col. Henry S. Burton having obtained necessary stores and two six pounders at Los Angeles, left San Pedro with his command of 110 men on the U. S. store-ship Lexington, to occupy the port of La Paz, Lower California. He had of the 1st N. Y. Regiment Company A, Capt. Seymour G. Steele and Company B, Capt. H. C. Matsell. After several conflicts the occupation was firmly established and maintained, until the troops were withdrawn and that country delivered over to Mexico under the terms of the Treaty. An episode of war, that has a glow of romance in more than one of its pleasing traditions. Lieut. Col. Burton afterward served on the Pacific Coast several years and in the Civil war. He died with the rank of Major General. His widow, Dona Ampara de Burton, and son Harry, and daughter Nellie reside in San Diego County. Capt. Steele is at Scott's Valley, Cal. Capt. Matsell afterward was a merchant at the city of San Diego; is living, it is believed, in New York. Of the privates in this daring service four are at Los Angeles: Messrs. Peter Thompson, James O'Sullivan, August Ehlers and Moses W. Perry.

Of the native Californians some probably dreamed of help to come from Mexico through their beloved Governor, Don Pio Pico. In August, 1846, he had set out for the capital, leaving them his assurance of re-inforcements. But by this time the better portion of the people had become convinced that further opposition must be unavailing. Their cherished institution—the Ayuntamiento (Town Council), which had closed its sessions July 4th, 1846, at the first sound of war—was restored in every detail according to their old laws. The familiar words *"Dios y Libertad"* (God and Liberty), authenticated their official communication among themselves as if the Mexican banner were flying. The election took place February 10th, 1847, the first meeting February 20th. Its members were: First Alcalde and President, Don Jose Salazar; Second Alcalde, Don Enrique Abila; Regidores (Council-men), Don Miguel N. Pryor, Don Rafael Gallardo, Don Julian Chavez, Don Jose Antonio Yorba; Sindico (Treasurer,) Don Jose Vicente Guerrero; Secretary, Don Ygnacio Coronel.

Its record is creditable to their probity, intelligence, economy and zeal for the public good. Owing to misunderstandings between this body and the military commandant, Col. Stevenson, at the end of December it was dissolved by Gov. Richard B. Mason, and January 1st, 1848, Stephen C. Foster as Alcalde by military appointment, took the place of the Ayuntamiento, with like jurisdiction over a wide stretch of country beyond the limits of the city. This office he held until May 21st of the ensuing year, displaying superior skill in its various and often difficult business. The Irrigation system every season had been a source of perplexity to the officers, and inconvenience and losses to the people, who never could find more than some temporary expedient to keep up the *toma* (dam) so necessary for the cultivation of the one hundred and three vineyards and gardens then existing. In February after his appointment, by a measure firmly executed at insignificant cost to each proprietor, he put it in a condition that was not disturbed until the great freshet of 1861—'62.

A thousand things combined to smooth the asperities of war. Fremont had been courteous and gay; Mason was just and firm. The natural good temper of the population favored a speedy and perfect conciliation. The American officers at once found themselves happy in every circle. In suppers, balls, visiting in town and country, the hours glided away with pleasing reflections. For hospitality the families were unrivalled through the world; and really were glad that it had not been worse at San Gabriel. "Men capable of such actions ought not to have been shot," they said in softest Castilian—admiring the American dash and daring displayed on that occasion. General Andres Pico and his *compadre* Lieutenant Stoneman, made the race against Sutler Sam Haight and a native turf-man—when Old Oso of the Picos and Workman, staked by the General and Lieutenant, beat Dr. Nicolas Den's "Champion of Santa Barbara," name forgotten, a thousand yards. On the other side a fascination seized them for the Queen of Angels. Army officers are believed to be no indifferent judges of wine. Dr. Griffin says the day after their entry—"It is of excellent flavor; as good as I ever tasted. The white wine is particularly fine. I ate of a fine orange. Taking everything into consideration this is decidedly one of the most desirable places I have ever been at." Camped on the sandy Santa Ana January 19th, on the return march to San Diego, thought turned back to this "very pleasant place —we found it so—we lived well and had the best of wine." At San Diego in December before, their reception had been if possible warmer from that ever enthusiastic and generous people. Don Juan Bandini and wife, Dona Refugio, had thrown open their mansion to the Commodore. All San Diego vied one with another to pay him honor and gild the flying moments with joy. Don Miguel Pedrorena and his relative, Don Santiago E. Arguello took up arms for the United States; both went with Commodore Stockton to Los Angeles. The inhabitants saw the army depart on the 29th in mingled sympathy and fear for the result. They welcomed all that returned to the wonted round of festivities. The Navy reciprocated the courtesy of the people. "On the 22nd, Washington's Birth-day," says Dr. Griffin, "the Commodore gave an elegant blow out on board of the Congress. The decorations were the flags of all nations; the ship's deck decidedly the gayest ball room I ever saw. We had all the ladies from San Diego. Everything went off in the happiest manner."

An investigation of the causes of misunderstanding between Col Stevenson and the Ayuntamiento before referred to, is of little importance at the present day. Probably it would not be unfavorable to the Ayuntamiento. Accounts from the best citizens concur, that the same confidence was felt in Col. Stevenson that had been displayed toward the other officers; as one expresses it, "all was harmony and pleasure." There were not wanting persons however who were not content to keep for themselves a bed of roses. Occasionally sentinels were disturbed or fancied so by false alarms, in one of which in December, 1847, a little after midnight preparing to load a cannon at the guard-house, situated on the hillside where is the mansion of Senator Bush, a careless soldier exploded a box of cartridges. Everything was thrown into the air—walls, soldiers; some of the timbers fell over into Main Street. Not one adobe was left standing upon another. Four were killed outright and twelve wounded, dragoons and men of Stevenson's regiment. It was immediately rebuilt of adobes. The accident is the more monstrous—this alarm having been produced by a sentinel who hailed a horse or cow grazing upon the hill, and for want of answer fired. Carefully inquiring among residents of that period and consulting the archives which are fully extant, not the slightest trace of any movement is visible among the Californians against the existing authorities, nor any real ground for suspicion or alarm at any time after January, 1847.

We may imagine something of the isolation and suspense of the American forces in California, through 1847, and later, from the accounts we have of the kind of intelligence received by them concerning events transpiring nearer the Capital of Mexico. May 6th, 1847—Dr. G. says: "Flying rumors are said to have reached Monterey that the Castle of San Juan de Ulloa has been taken, and that Taylor has had another fight, in which he was victorious." Lieut. Col. Burton, July 9th, brought news of General Scott's two victories of Vera Cruz and Puente Nacional—a salute was fired in consequence; and August 19th, "the Californians received, via. Sonora, the Mexican papers describing the movements of Scott and Taylor: the taking of Vera Cruz, and the battle of Puente Nacional." So, at the City of Los Angeles. Buenavista, on February 23d, had been the last battle of General Taylor. March 27th, Vera Cruz had surrendered. April 18th, Gen. Scott had stormed, successfully, Cerro Gordo; the next day he entered Jalapa, and the populous City of Puebla on the 15th of May. August 20th, Contreras and Churubuzco were carried. September 8th, Molino del Rey; 13th, Chapultepec; and, on the 15th, he took possession of the capital. At Guadalupe Hidalgo the Treaty was signed February 8th, and President Polk proclaimed peace on the 4th of July, 1848. Under the treaty the United States paid to Mexico $15,000,000.

The "Veterans of the Mexican War" were organized into a Society, at the City of Los Angeles, September 27th, 1873. The name and nativity of residents are as follows:

OFFICERS.—President, Gen. George H. Stoneman, New York; Vice Presidents, Peter Thompson, New York, and W. Todd, Illinois; Secretary, J. D. Dunlap, New Hampshire; Treasurer, G. W. Whitehorn, New York; Marshal, Capt. Wm. Turner, Isle of Wight.

EXECUTIVE COMMITTEE.—Fenton M. Slaughter, Virginia; Dr. William B. Dunne, Ireland; Geo. W. Cole, Illinois; G. W. Whitehorn, New York; Robert T. Johnson, Tennessee.

MEMBERS.—Province of Maine—Nelson Williamson, Joseph R. W. Hand. Maine—Stephen C. Foster, Albion C. Libby. New Hampshire—David M. Main. Vermont—Myron Norton. Rhode Island—Lewis A. Wilmot. New York—Edward E. Hewit, George Carson, James B. Caywood, Gabriel Allen, George Davis, Jas. H. Stewart, Abraham Maricole, Albert Clark. Pennsylvania—Henry C. Wiley, James F. Wilson. Maryland—Jonathan Knott, Ephraim Forbush, Joshua Talbott, John J. Mills, Thomas B. Wade, John F. Staples. District Columbia—Geo. Smith, George Diggs. Virginia—Dr. John S. Griffin, Thomas Enroughty, James W. Spratt, Archer C. Jessie, Pleasant Byas, William W. Brown. North Carolina —Robert C. Dobson, William C. Hughes, Lewis A. Green, Tennessee—Thomas J. Ash, Robert T. Johnson, Joseph Bridger, John T. Davis, Wm. T. Henderson, F. H. Alexander, Benjamin D. Wilson, James M. Smith, Anderson Wright. Kentucky—Charles M. Benbrook, James H. Easton, Pinckney C. Molloy, Shapley P. Ross, James Thompson, James W. B. Davis. Ohio—Wilson Bench, Charles Chancy, Isaih Smith, Gracia C. Norris, Marcus Serrott, Augustus C. Chauvan.

Illinois—Andrew J. Cole, Charles O'Niel. Georgia—Clement C. Goodwin, John P. H. Chew. Pauldo G. Rushmore. South Carolina—Allen W. Neighbors. Mississippi—Edward J. C. Kewen, Edward H. Cage. Indiana—James W. Taggart, F. M. Matthew. Ireland—Matthew St. Clair Gardner, David W. Alexander, Paul Ryan, Nicolas Keating, Michael Halpin. Canada—Elijah T. Moulton. England—John Roach, John V. Moore, William O. Baxter, Robert W. Allen. Germany—August Ehlers, John Shumacher, Augustus Tipple, Valentin Mand. Austria—Gotfried Voight. Russia—Alexander Saurwied. Prussia—Augustus W. Timms. Philipine Islands—William P. Reynolds.

Deceased members were Johan Carl Eserich, Andra Weinshank, John Reed, and Thomas Standifer—the last dying June, 1875.

The Treaty of Guadalupe Hidalgo was ratified May 30th, 1848. The news did not reach Los Angeles until August fifteenth. In the same month were celebrated the nuptials of Stephen C. Foster and Dona Merced Lugo, daughter of Don Antonio Maria Lugo. Don Antonio Maria died in 1860. He was born in 1775, at the Mssion of San Antonio de Padua. A link between two centuries—his name a household word throughout California. In the same month, or July, ex-Governor Don Pio Pico returned to Los Angeles from Guaimas, having effected nothing during his absence of two years. The Mexican Government neglected all his representations, and finally refused to permit him or his Secretary, Don Jose Matias Moreno, to visit the capital. It was a patriotic dream which he had indulged for his native land. The cold policy of Mexico seems to have parted with this remote region without a single regret. Don Pio has lived to a green old age, none the less honored for having been the last Mexican Governor of California. In September, Col. Stevenson left for San Francisco. January, 1849, a squadron of Second Dragoons, Major Montgomery Pike Graham commanding, fresh from Mexico, was posted at this city. His officers were: Captain Kane Quartermaster; Captain, D. H. Rucker; Lieutenants, Cave J. Couts, Givens, Sturgiss, Campbell, Evans, and Wilson. Captain Rufus Ingalls was here in this year as Quartermaster. The arrival of Major Graham relieved Company C, First Dragoons, which then marched for Sonoma, under its officers as before mentioned, and the Surgeon Dr. Griffin.

Commodore Robert Field Stockton was born at Princeton, New Jersey, in 1796; was distinguished by his naval services in the Mediterranean and other seas. California owes to him its first press and first public school house, under American rule. In 1851, he represented his native State in the U. S. Senate, and succeeded in having the passage of a law abolishing flogging in the navy. He died October 7th, 1866.

General Stephen Watts Kearny was born at Newark, New Jersey, Aug. 30th, 1794. In June, 1846, he was made Brigadier General in command of "the Army of the West," and took possession of New Mexico, established a provisional government, and marched for California. He died at Saint Louis, Missouri, October 31st, 1848.

Of the original command of General Kearny, Lieutenant Warner was killed at Goose Lake, in the northern part of this State, in 1849, by Indians. Captain William Emory is Major General, U. S. A. Lieutenant Stoneman is on the retired list, with the rank of Brevet Major General; resides on his farm near Los Angeles City. Lieutenant J. B. Davidson is Brevet Brigadier General. Major Thomas Swords, Quartermaster, is retired. Captain A. J. Smith was a General in and resigned after the Civil War. Captain Turner resigned after the Mexican War. Dr. Griffin resigned in 1854. Captain Turner became partner in the banking house of Lucas, Turner & Co., San Francisco—the same house with which General Sherman was connected, James R. Barton, Captain Alexander Bell, Daniel Sexton, and John Reed were of the volunteers with Kearny. Sexton resides at the City of San Bernardino. John Reed was First Sergeant of Captain Hensly's company, under Fremont, at the occupation of Los Angeles, August, 1846; he was born in North Carolina; died July 13th, 1875, aged 57 years, at his farm, Puente, in this county. He married the only daughter of John Roland; she survives him. John Carl Eschrich, so familiarly known to the Californians as "Don Carlos," of Stevenson's regiment, died at the age of 52 years, June 10th, 1871; he was a native of Germany. Don Miguel de Pedrorena died March 30th, 1850, in San Diego County. Don Santiago E. Arguello in 1859, at his Rancho La Punta, in same county. A soldier who served out of California, Andra Weinshank, born in Bavaria, died at this city February 16th, 1874, aged 54 years. He was at Vera Cruz, and all the battles on Scott's line. Elijah T. Moulton, of the Fremont battalion, resides at Los Angeles. Of the privates of Company C, First Dragoons, are resident at this city: George Washington Whitehorn, born at Pennington, Monroe County, New York, 1821; Wm. Burden Dunne, Cork, 1818; and in this county, Michael Halpin, born at Limerick, 1823. Company K, Lieutenant

Johnson commanding, and Company C, Captain Ben. Moore, formed the escort of General Kearny after leaving Rio Grande—the rest having been sent back at Socorro, on meeting Kit Carson, with despatches from Commodore Stockton, announcing the conquest of California. The day before the battle on San Pascual Johnston was promoted to a Captaincy. On December 7th, before the march from the battle ground, the men of Company K were incorporated into Company C. On Christmas eve, 1846, Don Pedro C. Carrillo sailed from San Diego with Captain Hamly (of the whaling ship Stonington), on the brig Malcck-Adel, as bearers of despatches to Fremont, who was expected to be found at Santa Barbara. He was Receptor (Collector) of San Diego, under the Mexican authority, when Captain Dupont, in the sloop of war Cyane, took that port. He was then appointed Judge of First Instance of San Diego District. In 1847, he was made U. S. Collector of Santa Barbara; in 1848, Judge of First Instance of that District. In 1851, he represented Santa Barbara County in the Assembly of this State; the same year he was appointed, by President Pierce, Surveyor of Customs for Santa Barbara, which office he held until 1861. He resides at Los Angeles City.

This civic-military rule lasted from January 1st, 1848, to May 21st, 1849. On the 17th of that month, under an order of Maj. Graham, Los Angeles ceased to be a military station of the United States. The new Ayuntamiente was inaugurated on the 21st. Its members were: First Alcalde and President, Don Jose del Carmen Lugo; Second Alcalde, Don Juan Sepulveda, Regidores, Don Jose Lopez, Don Francisco Ruis, Don Francisco O'Campo, Don Tomas A. Sanchez; Sindico, Don Juan Temple; Secretary, Don Jesus Guirado. "Ord's Survey" of the city and other well conceived measures attest their usefulness. Their successors holding from January 2nd to June 29th, 1850, were: First Alcalde and President, Abel Stearns; Second Alcalde, Ignacio del Valle; Regidores, David W. Alexander, Benjamin D. Wilson, Jose L. Sepulveda, Manuel Garfias; Sindico, Francisco Figueroa; Secretary, Jesus Guirado. Upon going out of office as Alcalde in 1849, Stephen C. Foster was appointed Prefect by Governor Bennett Riley. This was a stormy period for officers of the city; the records show that their duty was well performed. To the care of Prefect Foster and Alcalde Stearns then— and to the first named gentleman since—are we much indebted for the preservation of the city and county archives, and for the admirable order of arrangement in which they are found.

From the year 1836, or a year or two before, Mr. Stearns had always figured through their local administrations, in one manner or another, beneficially to the people. He was born at Salem, Massachusetts; spent considerable time in Mexico; came to Los Angeles in 1828; his business a merchant. His fortune seems to have begun about 1842. He obtained several large grants of land, in this county and elsewhere. He was a member of the Constitutional Convention of 1849, and of the State Legislature; always a prominent and useful citizen until his death, at San Francisco, August 23d, 1871, at the age of 72 years. He married Dona Arcadia, daughter of Don Juan Bandini. Dona Ysidora, daughter of Don Juan, was married to Colonel Cave J. Couts April 4th, 1851. Colonel C. is before mentioned as Lieutenant in Major Graham's command. Col. C. resigned his commission in November following; established the Rancho of Guajome, in San Diego County. He died wealthy, at the City of San Diego, June 10th, 1874, leaving his widow, four daughters, and four sons. Don Juan Bandini came to California in 1819, and for many years filled a considerable space in the public view. He was *Administrador* of the Mission San Gabriel in 1839; one of the Ayuntamiento of Los Angeles in 1844; member of the Departmental Assembly at its suspension, on the approach of the U. S. forces, August 10th, 1846, but at that date was at home in San Diego. He had partly written a history of California at the time of his death, which took place at this city, November 2d, 1859, at the age of fifty-nine years. He was a profound thinker, a clear, forcible writer. Don Juan was twice married; his first wife, Dona Dolores Estudillo, daughter of Don Jose Estudillo, formerly the distinguished military commander of Montery; his second, Dona Refugio Arguello. Both ladies possessed singular beauty. Of the first marriage, are Mrs. Robert S. Baker, Mrs. Couts, Mrs. Pedro C. Carillo, and two sons, Jose Maria Bandini and Juanito Bandini. Of the second, are Mrs. Charles R. Johnson, Mrs. Dr. James B. Winston, and three sons, Juan de la Cruz Bandini, Alfredo Bandini, and Arturo Bandini.

It was a pretty incident—the manufacture of the first American flag on this Pacific Coast. On arriving at San Diego, in the Fall of 1846, Commodore Stockton, awhile, was kept almost in a state of siege. Beef was indispensable for immediate demand, and beef, horses, and work-oxen, for further operations by land. Don Juan Bandini then was at his Rancho of Guadalupe, eighty miles south of San Diego. In order to secure necessary supplies a strong force, under Major Hensly, was sent into Lower California; and at Guadalupe obtained 500 head of cattle, 200 horses, and eight carretas, drawn by oxen. Don Juan and family accompanied him on the return march. Joyfully all had reached La Punta, within fifteen miles of San Diego, when the Major observed that he was without a flag to crown his triumphal entry into the post. Woman's thought is equal to an emergency. Dona Refugio offered to work one on the spot. Little Dolores (Mrs. Johnson) and smaller Margarita (Mrs. Winston) wore the red and blue—white soon came to hand—and an impromptu Star-Spangled Banner, perfect as ever floated in air,cheered the rest of the march. That night, a serenade to the fair maker, from all the grand music of Congress and Savannah, celebrated the event, and the third day thereafter the gift was acknowledged, in person, by Commodore and officers. Impressively, as he always promised, he said to that amiable lady: " Whatever you may ask of the United States, it shall be granted." Although she believes she has just claims, they remain unrequited.

Her father whom we have before mentioned, Don Santiago Arguello, was born at Monterey, son of Don Jose Dario Arguello, Governor of both Californias, and brother of Don Jose Arguello, who was afterward Governor of Alta California. Don Santiago married Dona Pilar Ortega, of Santa Barbara, both very young, there being two years difference in their ages. They had twenty-two children. He died November 7th, 1862, at the age of 74 years. Five children survive, and Dona Pilar, with a very large number of grand children and great grand children. Dona Conception, one of their daughters, was married to Don Agustin Olvera. One of their grand daughters is the wife of Capt. A. H. Wilcox of San Diego; another of W. B. Couts, Esq., of San Luis Rey. Dona Teresa the only other daughter who survives,is married to Don Jose Maria Bandini of Tia Juana rancho, Lower California, where also resides the venerable widow.

The Constitutional Convention of this State, adopted the Constitution, October 10th., 1849; it was ratified by vote of the people, November 13th., and proclaimed by Gov. Riley, December 13th. Besides Mr. Stearns, Los Angeles was represented by Don Jose Antonio Carrillo, Perfecto Hugo Reid, Stephen C. Foster, and Don Manuel Dominguez. Don Manuel had honorably filled several responsible stations prior to 1846. He often visits the City. Mr. Reid died at Los Angeles December 12th, 1852. He was a native of Scotland, of great intelligence, and always held in high esteem. He wrote some essays on the history, customs, and legends of the Los Angeles Indians, and vocabularies of several Indian tongues spoken in this section of the State, which have been published. Don Jose Antonio Carrillo died at Santa Barbara, April 25th, 1862, aged 67 years.

The first County election was held April 1st. 1850. Three hundred and seventy-seven votes were cast in the county. The officers chosen were: County Judge, Agustin Olvera; County Clerk, Benj. Davis Wilson; County Attorney, Benj. Hayes; County Surveyor, J. R. Conway; County Treasurer, Manuel Garfias; County Assessor, Antonio F. Coronel; County Recorder, Ignacio del Valle; County Sheriff, George T. Burrill; County Coroner, Charles B. Cullen.

Don Agustin Olvera, when elected County Judge, was "Juez de 1a Instancia"—Judge of First Instance—of the Los Angeles District, under appointment of Gov. Riley. He emigrated to California from the City of Mexico, and arrived September 16th, 1834. There came at the same time Don Ignacio Coronel, his wife Dona Francisca Romero, two sons Don Antonio Franco Coronel and Don Manuel Coronel and four daughters. His sons have been and still are among our prominent citizens. They formed a part of the celebrated expedition of Don Jose Maria Hijar and Don Jose Maria Padres, which had been organized with infinite care for colonization in California, especial view being had to select men of character,intelligence

3

and some useful occupation. It consisted of lawyers, physicians, printers, carpenters, tanners, saddlers, shoemakers, hatters, tailors, laborers, and a confectioner. Don Joaquin de los Rios y Rios was a surgeon of repute in Los Angeles and San Diego for several years after 1840, until his death. Don Francisco Torres, another physician, returned to Mexico. Don Ignacio Coronel was one of its school-masters; taught in this city for a long time; afterward confined himself to the duties of Secretary of the Ayuntamiento; subsequently was a Justice of the Peace. Education was especially provided for by the Mexican Government in this colony. The Missions had just been secularized; the formation of *Pueblos* was therefore contemplated. Accordingly experienced teachers were sent for the Public Schools to be established at each Mission; which measure took effect at the Missions of Santa Clara, San Jose, San Gabriel and San Luis Rey; also at Monterey, and in the year 1838 at Los Angeles. At the organization, in the year 1841, of the Pueblo of San Juan de Arguello—so named in honor of Don Santiago Arguello—which is generally called San Juan Capistrano—Don Agustin Olvera was appointed "Juez de Paz" of that jurisdiction, from Santa Ana to Las Flores. He resided there in 1842, 1843, 1844. It is spoken of as a well ordered place, with an industrious, contented population. Don Agustin was admitted as attorney in this the then 1st. Judicial District, in 1853, and April 11th, 1855, in the U. S. District Court, in 1856, he was the Receiver of the Los Angeles U. S. Land Office. At the taking of the city, in 1846, he was a member of the Departmental Assembly; as such member, acted as one of the Commissioners in the Cahuenga negotiation. Don Jose Antonio Carrillo, the other Mexican Commissioner, held the rank of Major General. Don Ignacio Coronel, born in the city of Mexico, died at Los Angeles city, at an advanced age, December 19, 1862.

Jonathan R. Scott was the first Justice of the Peace, merely taking that office in order to give his ability to the county organization. He soon tired of it and was succeeded by J. S. Mallard. Judge Scott had been a prominent lawyer in Missouri and was in the front rank of the Bar at Los Angeles. He was ready for any useful enterprise. In company with Mr. Abel Stearns he built the first brick flouring mill in 1855, and about two years before his death he planted an extensive vineyard. He died September 21st, 1864. His eldest daughter married A. B. Chapman, Esq. His only son has recently been admitted to the Bar. His widow of a second marriage and family reside in this city.

The early lawyers arriving in the order mentioned were: Don Manuel C. Rojo, 1849; Russell Sackett, 1849; Louis Granger, 1850; Benj. Hayes, Feb. 3, 1850; Jonathan R. Scott, March, 1850. The last four as well as Mr. Hartman were overland emigrants. Law books were scarce. A brief passage in "Kent's Commentaries" that was found somewhere in town, decided an interesting case between the rich Peruvian passenger and liberal French sea-captain, sometime in March, before First Alcalde Stearns. The Captain lost, but comforted his attorney, Scott, with a thousand dollar fee, as it happened, all in five dollar gold pieces. In 1850 also came Wm. G. Dryden and J. Lancaster Brent, the latter with a good library; 1851, I. K. S. Ogier, Ogier & Rojo, May 31, 1851; 1852, Myron Norton, James H. Lander, Charles E. Carr, Ezra Drown, Columbus Sims, Kimball H. Dimmick, Henry Hancock, Isaac Hartman; 1853, Samuel R. Campbell; 1854, Cameron E. Thom and James A. Watson, ("Col. Jack Watson"); E. J. C. Kewen, W. W. Hamlin, 1856; Alfred B. Chapman, 1858; Volney E. Howard, 1861; Andrew J. Glassell and Col. James G. Howard arrived on the same steamer, November 27th, 1865, from San Francisco. Myers J. Newmark was admitted to the Bar in September, and Andrew J. King in October, 1859; Don Ignacio Sepulveda, September 6th, 1862. Henry T. Hazard, son of Ariel M. Hazard, of Evanston, near Chicago, since when about eight years of age has always resided in this city, except about six years of absence at College. He is a graduate of the University of Michigan, was admitted to the Bar in that State in 1867, and the following year in California. Other attorneys prior to 1860 were Hon. S. F. Reynolds (afterward District Judge of San Francisco), Joseph R. Gitchell (in April, 1858, appointed District Attorney), A. Thomas, William E. Pickett, Casaneuva & Jones advertised December 13, 1851. This was William Claude

Jones, known so well in Missouri. Scott & Hayes were partners from March, 1850, until April 13th, 1852; afterward Scott & Granger; then Scott & Lander. Between 1852 and 1860 the Land Questions before the Commissioners and U. S. District Court brought almost as residents distinguished lawyers— H.W.Halleck, A. C. Peachy, F. Billings, C.B.Strode,Wm. Carey Jones, P. W. Tompkins, Gregory Yale, John H. Saunders, H. P. Hepburn, not to name others. There are dead Russell Sackett, 1872; James H. Lander, Ezra Drown, Columbus Sims; Kimball H. Dimmick, 1856; James A. Watson, S. R. Campbell; Clarke, at New Orleans; Carr, at Washington City; Joseph R. Gitchell, 1866. J. Lancaster Brent stood high as a lawyer and Statesman. He resides in Louisiana, near New Orleans, and in part represented that State in the late Democratic National Convention at St. Louis. Mr. Granger was a fluent, pretty speaker; in 1852-3, partner of Judge Scott; recently candidate for Judge of the First Judicial District. Gen. Drown lost his wife in the stranding of the steamer Independence. He died August 17th, 1863, leaving a son:—as a man much thought of, and very successful in his profession. Hon. K. H. Dimmick, a Captain in Colonel Stevenson's regiment, had been a member of the Constitutional Convention of 1849. James H. Landers was born March 10th, 1829, at New York City. He was a graduate of Harvard. He was an excellent office lawyer. For a long time he was Court Commissioner, with especial approbation of the Bar. October 15th, 1852 he married Miss Margarita Johnson, a daughter of Don Santiago Johnson, so well remembered among the early business men of this coast before 1846. A son and daugter survive, of this marriage. In 1872 he married Miss Mollie E. Holden, of Baltimore, Md. They had one daughter, who with her mother lives at Los Angeles. He died June 10th, 1873. Samuel R. Campbell was born near Nashville, Tenn.; died in San Bernardino county early in January 1863, or about the last of December 1862, near fifty years of age. He practiced law for a long time in Andrew county, Mo. His memory was most extraordinary. A poem or oration once read to him, or read by him, he could repeat word for word years afterward. He was in the habit, when familiarly illustrating this faculty, to recite in full, page after page of Blackstone's Commentaries. His widow and children reside in this city. His son, Thornton P. Campbell, is a merchant and member of the City Council. Of the living all reside within the city, save Col. E. J. C. Kewen and General Volney E. Howard; nay, early the railway brings them to the forum, both from classic villas eight miles away, one of the ancient Mission of San Gabriel.

Col. James A. Watson, October 13th, 1855, married Miss Dolores Dominguez. He died at this city, September 16th, 1869, aged forty-five years. The latter part of his life was devoted to his vineyard and orchard. He had been a skillful politician, and was esteemed as a lawyer.

Hon. Myron Norton was born September 23d, 1822, at Bennington, Vt. He studied law in New York, was admitted to the Bar in 1844, continued in practice at Troy until 1848, when he was appointed first Lieutenant of California volunteers, and in the Summer of that year arrived at Monterey. He was a member of the Constitutional Convention from San Francisco; afterward Judge of the Superior Court of San Francisco. In 1855 he was the Democratic candidate for Judge of the Supreme Court of this State. He dwells in the agreeable family of Don Agustin Olvera, and not entirely withdrawn from business. Don Manuel Clemente Rojo, our first *abogado*, (lawyer) is a native of Peru, of finished education and excellent qualities of head and heart. A few years ago he was Sub-Political Chief of the Frontier of Lower California, and is practicing his profession there with marked distinction. An old emigrant named Williams, throwing out of his wagon almost everything else, saved his son's law library. They reached John Roland's in December, 1849, the ambitious young attorney with his eye to the polar star. Roland, in his usual liberal style, outwitted complete son and father. It is not known how fortune may have dealt with them since.

Sheriff Burrill of 1850, was punctilious, perhaps formal, but affable; and pleasantly conspicuous by the infantry dress sword which he wore in public thrown his term, as he said, according to official custom of Mexico, where he had lived a good while. His brother is author of the "Law Glossary." He was hero of a "scene in Court," one bright afternoon in the Summer of 1850. Judge Witherby was hearing an application for bail, on a charge of murder against three native Californians. The large room is not to be recognized, with the changes of the Bella Union. Upon a side bench together sat the prisoners. The Judge, Thomas W. Sutherland (acting District Attorney), Benj. Hayes (County Attorney), Clerk—and counsel, J. Lancaster Brent; present, none others—save twelve, fierce, determined fellows, "armed to the teeth," huddled up in the far corner. Preliminaries disposed of—calm content smoothed the face of Sheriff B., that sword by his side, when appeared eighteen of the 1st Dragoons, at the critical moment. They dismounted, tied their horses to the Celis balcony—Lafayette now—and fell into line in front of the building. Bond approved, a Sargeant led the accused outside, placed them on horseback between his files, and so conducted them home: a pin might have been heard to drop, and in the stillness, the Court adjourned. Major E. H. Fitzgerald had encamped the night before, on the edge of town. This was the *posse* put at the service of Sheriff B., and that left him pleased infinitely at its effect, almost like a charm, upon this famous "Irving party" in the corner. By the by, Los Angeles Sheriffs have many an interesting incident in their careers—David W. Alexander, 1855, and others.   Mr. Burrill died Feb. 2d, 1856.

California was admitted into the Union September 9th, 1850. Some of of the principal offices, since 1850, have been filled as follows: District Judge—Oliver S. Witherby, three years; Benjamin Hayes, eleven years; Pablo de la Guerra, Murray Morrison, R. M. Widney; Ignacio Sepulveda, 1876. County Judge—Agustin Olvera, four years; Myron Norton, Kimball H. Dimmick, William G. Dryden, Andrew J. King, Ignacio Sepulveda; H. K. S. O'Melveny, 1876. County Clerk—Benjamin D. Wilson, Wilson W. Jones, Charles R. Johnson, John W. Shore, Thomas D. Mott, Stephen H. Mott; A. W. Potts, 1876.   Sheriff—George T. Burrill, David W. Alexander, James R. Barton, Wm. C. Getman, James R. Barton, (murdered Friday, Jan. 23d, 1857, while in the discharge of official duty), Tomas A. Sanchez, James F. Burns, William R. Roland; D. W. Alexander, 1876.   Wm. Getman died January 7th, 1858.   County Treasurer—Manuel Garfias, now American Consul, Tepic, Mexico; Timothy Foster, Henry N. Alexander, Morice Kremer, Thomas E. Rowan; Francis P. F. Temple, 1876. District Attorney—William C. Ferrel, now a mountain farmer of Lower California; Isaac S. K. Ogier, Sept. 29th, 1851; Kimball H. Dimmick, appointed July 10th, elected November 29th, 1852; Benjamin S. Eaton, October 3d, 1853; Cameron E. Thom, October 3d, 1854; Ezra Drown, Alfred B. Chapman, Volney E. Howard, A. B. Chapman, C. E. Thom, V. E. Howard; Rodney Hudson, 1876.   County Assessor—Antonio F. Coronel, 1850-1856; Juan Sepulveda, 1857-1858; W. W. Maxy, 1859-1860; J. McManus, 1861; G. L. Mix, 1862-1864; J. Q. A. Stanly, 1865-1866; Manuel F. Coronel, 1867-1868; 1869-1875, Dionisio Boteller; Andrew Ryan, 1876.   County Recorder—Ignacio del Valle, 1850-1851; (Recorder and County Clerk united); J. W. Gillett, March 1st, Monday, 1874; Charles E. Miles, March 1st, Monday, 1876.   Court Commissioner (District)—George Clinton Gibbs.

The present County officers not above just mentioned are: Under Sheriff—H. Milner Mitchell. Deputy Sheriffs—Wm. L. Banning, Emil Harris. Deputy County Clerks—E. H. Owen, D. W. Maclellan. Deputy County Treasurer—E. M. Spence. Deputy Recorder—George E. Gard. Auditor—Andronico E. Sepulveda. Tax Collector—Morice Kremer. County Surveyor—T. J. Ellis. Deputy Assessors—M. Ryan, W. H. A. Kidd. Coroner—Dr. Joseph Kurtz. School Superintendent—Thomas A. Saxon. Supervisors—Geo. Hines (Chairman), Gabriel Allen, Edward Evy, John D. Young, J. C. Hannon. Justices of the Peace (city)—John Trafford, Pedro C. Carrillo, William H. Gray.

Don Ignacio Sepulveda, present District Judge, is a native of this city. He was educated in the East. Oliver Spencer Witherby was born at Cincinnati, Ohio, Feb. 19th, 1815; Benj. Hayes at Baltimore, Md. Feb. 14th, 1815; Robert M. Widney, Miami county, Ohio, December 23d, 1838.

Don Pablo de la Guerra was born in the Presidio of Santa Barbara, November 29th, 1819. He was State Senator four terms from the district of Santa Barbara and San Luis Obispo, and had been a member of the Constitutional Convention of 1849. His term of District Judge commenced January 1st, 1864. He died February 5th, 1874, having a short time before resigned the Judgship of the first District, in consequence of ill health.

Hon. Murray Morrison was born at Kaskaskia, Illinois, in 1820; was admitted to the Bar in 1842. In 1862 he married Miss Jennie White, daughter of Dr. Thomas J. White. In 1868, on the creation of the 17th Judicial District, he was appointed Judge by Gov. Haight; and elected in 1869. He died at this city December 18th, 1871. Within three days a loving wife followed him to the tomb.

Hon. Wm. G. Dryden, November 30th, 1851, married Miss Dolores Nieto. His second wife was Miss Anita Dominguez, daughter of Don Manuel Dominguez; married September 30th, 1868. He died at this city, aged 70 years, September 10th, 1869.

The Board to settle private land claims, organized in this city October, 1852. Commissioners—Hiland Hall, since Governor of Vermont; Harry I. Thornton, Thompson Campbell. It expired in 1855. Robert Greenhow first, then Gen. Volney E. Howard, then John H. McKune have been Law Agents of the United States; Cameron E. Thom Assistant Law Agent, in 1854. In some of the subsequent land cases before the United States District Court, Isaac Hartman was Special Attorney, in 1857, under Attorney General Black, and, in 1861, under Attorney General Bates. The United States District Court for the Southern District of California was instituted in December, 1855, Hon. John M. Jones, Judge; Pablo de la Guerra, Marshal; Alfred Wheeler, District Attorney; Samuel Flower, Clerk. Judge Jones died November 14th, of that year. In September, 1854, Edward Hunter was appointed Marshal in place of Pablo de la Guerra, resigned. Judge Ogier succeeded Judge Jones. Hon. Fletcher M. Haight succeeded Judge Ogier, and died at San Francisco shortly after the abolition of the Court by Act of Congress, passed in 1866. As District Attorney, Ogier succeeded Wheeler; then Pacificus Ord; then J. R. Gitchell.

Hon. Isaac Stockton Keith Ogier, for several years Judge, was born at Charleston, S. C., May 24th, 1817. He came to California in the year 1849. He died at Holcombe Valley, May 21st, 1861. His widow resides at this city.

The officers of the United States are: Postmaster—H. K. W. Bent. Register of the Land Office—Alfred James. Receiver—J. W. Haverstick. Guager—J. R. Brierly. Deputy Marshal—J. D. Dunlap. U. S. Commissioner—B. C. Whiting.

Gov. John G. Downey came to Los Angeles in December, 1850. He married Miss Maria Jesus Guirado, of this city, February 10th, 1852. His distinguished career belongs to the history of California.

In 1850 this county was represented in the State Senate by Dr. A. W. Hope; followed in 1851 and 1852 by Stephen C. Foster. The Senators since have been: 1853, 1854, James P. McFarland; 1855, 1856, Benjamin D. Wilson; 1857, 1858, Cameron E Thom; 1859, 1860, Andres Pico; 1861, 1862, John R. Vineyard; 1863, 1864, Henry Hamilton; 1865 until 1868, Phineas Banning; 1869 until 1872, B. D. Wilson; 1873 and now, C. W. Bush.

Members of Assembly—1850, A. P. Crittenden, Montgomery Martin. 1851, Abel Stearns, Ignacio del Valle. 1852, James P. McFarland, Capt. Jefferson Hunt. 1853, Charles E. Carr, Edward Hunter. 1854, Francis Mellus, Dr. Wilson W. Jones. 1855, John G. Downey, J. Lancaster Brent. 1856, J. Lancaster Brent, Edward Hunter. 1857, Andres Pico, Henry Hancock. 1858, Andres Pico, Henry Hancock. 1859, John J. Warner, Andrew J. King. 1860, Abel Stearns, Murray Morrison. 1861, James A. Watson, Murray Morrison. 1862, James A. Watson, Edward J. C. Kewen. 1863, 1864, Ignacio Sepulveda, E. J. C. Kewen. 1865, 1866, William H. Peterson, E. C. Parrish. 1867, 1868, Asa Ellis, James A. Watson. 1869, 1870, Manuel F. Coronel, R. C. Fryer. 1871, 1872, Thomas D. Mott, Asa Ellis. 1873, 1874, J. W. Venable, A. Higbie. 1875, 1876, John R. McConnell, Frederick Lambourne.

The City of Los Angeles was incorporated by Act of the Legislature, approved April 4th, 1850. The government was organized July 3d. Mayor,

A. P. Hodges; Common Council, David W. Alexander, President; Alexander Bell, Manuel Riquena, John Temple, Morris L. Goodman, Cristobal Aguilar, Julian Chavez. Recorder, John G. Nichols: Treasurer, Francisco Figueroa; Assessor, Antonio F. Coronel; Marshall, Samuel Whiting; Attorney, Benjamin Hayes.

The Mayors since have been, Benjamin D. Wilson, 1851; John G. Nichols, 1852; Antonio Franco Coronel, 1853; Stephen C. Foster, 1854; Thomas Foster, 1855; Stephen C. Foster, 4 months—John G. Nichols, residue, 1856; John G. Nichols, 1857, 1858; Damien Marchessault, 1859; Henry Mellus, 1860; D. Marchessault, 1861, 1862, 1863,1864; Jose Mascarel, 1865-'66; Cristobal Aguilar, 1867-'68; Joel Turner, 1869-'70; Cristobal Aguilar, 1871-'72; James R. Toberman, 1873-'74; Prudent Beaudry, 1875—.

Mayors Hodges and Wilson, through tempestuous times, held the helm with firmness and foresight. Under the first term of Nichols began Henry Hancock's survey. August 13th, 1852, is the date of the Donation System (repealed in 1854), by which thirty-five acre tracts and other lots were granted on sole condition of improvement, with payment of fees. He was Mayor again in 1857 and 1858. The uncertainty, apathy, rather, of the public mind upon the vital question of irrigation may be inferred from a remark in his message of the former year: "It appears that under the present system of irrigation there is as much land under cultivation as can be supplied with water from the river of the pueblo; but it is believed by our most intelligent farmers, and by many gentlemen of experience who have visited us, that by the adoption of a different system, a sufficiency of water to irrigate the entire plain below the city could be obtained." But on August 2d, 1858, Zanja No. 2 was provided for, which led to the building of Aliso Mill, and has brought a large amount of first rate land into cultivation. The survey was long before that, of Captain, now General E. O. C. Ord, to ascertain the practicability of bringing water for drinking and general domestic uses from the river over the bench land; a project supported by the business men, but defeated at the municipal election by an absurd prejudice and superior influence of leading vineyardists. To resume: Coronel had his hands full. The bulk of Donation lots was made by him. Stephen C. Foster managed well through 1854. In January, 1855,he resigned; within two weeks was re-elected without opposition; merely a curious circumstance, or a capricious freak, it might seem, if left unexplained.

October 13th, 1854, one David Brown killed Pinckney Clifford, in this city. This act created deep excitement. A public meeting on the next day was appeased only by the Mayor's promise that if the laws should fail, he would resign and help to punish the murderer. Brown was tried November 30th. The District Court—Benj. Hayes, Judge—sentenced him to be executed on the 12th day of January, 1855. The same day had been fixed by that Court for the execution of Felipe Alvitre, for the murder of James Ellington, in El Monte. In Brown's case, his counsel, J. R. Scott and J. A. Watson, had obtained from the Supreme Court a stay of execution. Public expectation waited for it, but a like stay did not come for the wretched, friendless Alvitre. This still more inflamed the native Californian and Mexican portion of the population. The fatal day arrived, and with it an early gathering at the county jail of a great multitude of all classes. Meanwhile, the Mayor had resigned. Sheriff Barton posted within the yard an armed guard of forty men. Alvitre was hung——the rope broke, he fell to the ground. *Arriba! Arriba!* (up! up!) was the cry from outside—all was instantly adjusted and the law's sentence carried into effect. Words fail to describe the demeanor then of that mass of eager, angry men. Suspense was soon over. Persuaded by personal friends—and in truth the odds against him seemed too great—Sheriff Barton withdrew the guard. The gate was crushed with heavy timbers, blacksmiths procured, the iron doors, locked and well barred from within, were forced. Within the next hour Brown was dragged from his cell to a corral across the street; where, amidst the shouts of the people, he uttered some incoherent observations, but quickly was hung from a beam of the corral gate. It is stated credibly, that a week thereafter was received an order of the Supreme Court, in favor of Alvitre, which had been delayed partly by the bad mail arrangements of that time, and more by reason of his appli cation having been first forwarded to the Governor. Another cell held a third person condemned for a later day; him the infuriated crowd did not molest. He was finally allowed a new trial by the Supreme Court, and at Santa Barbara acquitted.

Thomas Foster succeeded in May of this year. June 19th he signed the first well matured ordinance for establishing and regulating Common Schools. The first Public School houses were erected; and measures now were seriously fomented to increase the supply of water for agricultural and industrial pursuits in the South-western portion of the city. He died on his way to San Francisco, Jan. 28th, 1862. He was a native of Kentucky. Re-elected in 1856, Stephen C. Foster, after four months, resigned in order to attend to his executorship of the large estate of Col. Isaac Williams; the balance of his term being filled by J. G. Nichols, whose subsequent administration has been already referred to. Marchessault added the finishing touch to the Market House—present Court House—Sept. 30th, 1859. Through his subsequent terms he encouraged plans for a better supply of drinking water by the Sansevaine contract and improvement of the city dam; and also promoted Common Schools. He was born at Montreal, Canada; died January 20th, 1868, aged forty-seven years. Henry Mellus died, forty-five years of age, December 27th, 1860—his official career an image of his own personal suavity and honor. Mascarel signed the ordinance against carrying concealed weapons, and a grant of lands to the Pioneer Oil company. Aguilar approved the ample grant to the Canal and Reservoir company and opening of the Woolen Mill ditch, improvements of streets, Wilmington railroad, a new ordinance for obtaining title to city lands. Turner confirmed the old Mexican pueblo concession of Don Antonio Ignacio Abila; created the city Board of Education April 24th, 1869; provided for Commercial street extension to Alameda, July 29th; the three wards, and settlement of controversies with the Canal and Reservoir company. Toberman reduced the debt $30,000 and left near that amount in the Treasury; brought down taxes from $1.60 to $1.00 upon each hundred dollars of valuation. Since the charter of 1874, city legislation has been fruitful of measures which we leave, together with many of prior date omitted above, to take up the thread of travel through labrynths of the remoter past.

The discovery of "The Mines" in the year 1848, carried away many of the native population; created a new demand for the horses and cattle which the rancheros could so amply supply; brought a multitude of emigrants from Sonora, as well as from the United States; left the people at home here in a state of perpetual exaltation and excitement. During the summer of 1849 and winter and spring of 1850, Los Angeles was a thoroughfare of travel. Few could be induced to stop long. Every head was turned toward El Dorado. Through the summer of 1850 thirty Americans could be counted, and most of these without families. With or without means the in-comers had crowded forward; seldom destitute, for their necessities when known had met a generous response from the bounty of the 'Lugo family' at San Bernardino, a Williams at Chino, a Rowland and a Workman at La Puente. Nor only from these—Native Californian liberality everywhere opened its full hand to the way worn-stranger.

With the people of Los Angeles 1850 was a year of enjoyment, rather than of earnest pursuit of riches. Money was abundant. All sought to make the most of the pleasures of life, as it seemed.

They were passionately fond of the turf. They might justly boast of their horses, which had sometimes drawn applause at the capital of Mexico. Now and for many successive years they gave full play to this passion. August 16th, 1851, Don Pio Pico and compadre Teodosio Yorba gave their printed challenge "to the North" with bold defiance—"the glove is thrown down, let him who will take it up"—for a nine mile race, or four and a half and repeat, the stake 1,000 head of cattle worth $20 per head, and $2,000 in money; with a codicil, as it were, for two other races, one of two leagues out and back, the other of 500 varas—$2,000 and 200 head of full grown cattle bet on each race. March 21st following the nine mile heat was run two miles south of the city, between the Sydney mare, Black Swan, backed by Don Jose Sepulveda, and the California horse, Sarco, staked by Don Pio

Pico and Don Teodosio, the challengers. The mare won by 75 yards in 19 minutes and 20 seconds. Sarco the previous spring had run 9 Mexican miles in 18 minutes, 46 seconds. Not less than $50,000 must have changed hands. More deserves to be said of what the Californians tell of this exciting race. April 2nd the American mare, Nubbins, beat the American horse, Bear Meat, on the Wolfskill track by ten feet—distance 400 yards—for 400 cows. The year before Don Jose Sepulveda's California horse beat Don Pio's American horse half a length, for $2,000 in money and 500 head of cattle. Probably the *carera* is still talked of, of November 20th, 1851, at Santa Barbara, when Francisco Noriega's horse, Buey de Tango, beat Alfred Robinson's horse, Old Breeches, with a change of $20,000 among hands. In September, 1852, Don Andres Pico and Don Jose Sepulveda had two races, one for $1,000, the other for $1,600 and 300 head of cattle. October 20th was the exciting day of Don Jose's favorite, Canelo, backed by Don Fernando Sepulveda, and Alisan, a Santa Barbara horse, backed by Don Andres Pico—for 300 head of cattle and $1,600 a side; 400 yards; Canelo came out winner half a length. The New Years Ball at Don Abel Stearns' "where all the beauty and elegance of the city," says the editor in mellifluous Spanish, "contributed that night to give splendor to the dance," was followed on the tenth by two races. The end of Lent and all the grander festivals were partly enjoyed in this way. January 20th, 1853, was to be run the race of Ito, brought seven hundred miles, against Fred. Coy, stake $10,000. The natives were cautious and it was forfeited; but in March Moore & Brady's horse John Smith beat Powell's mare Sarah Jane for $2,100, by about a length. April 12, Buckhorne, an American horse, was led through the streets, gaily decked off as a banter; Don Pio Pico offered to back him against any nag in this part of the State; no takers." quoth the Star. Not to be disappointed of sport, on the 19th, they had Don Jose Sepulveda's horse Muchacho against Moore's *mule* for $550 a side: the horse won! In February 1857, Don Jose Sepulveda's horse Pinto easily beat Don Pio's Dick Johnson at San Gabriel, for $3000;and March 5th, Don Jose beat the Gonzales brothers at San Fernando for $2,000. Through the later years heavier stakes than any we have mentioned were lost and won by Don Juan Abila and others, except, perhaps, that of Black Swan and Sarco. Of a very early day some of the races occupy many pages of the archives. ,One tasked the best ability, as Alcalde, of the venerable Don Manuel Dominguez; one drew out a profound decision of Don Jose Antonio Carrillo, of the Supreme Court. The Governor did not disdain to lay down rules for racing. In his manuscript diary we have the authority of Mr. Francis Mellus, visiting Los Angeles from one of the Boston ships at San Pedro, for the race of Mose Carson, brother of Kit Carson, on January 20th, 1840. Mose had a heavy bet on two races for that day. The first he won, despite the salt that—for luck—had been put in all the holes of the stakes on the course, and of the little bag of salt and wax candle and silk cotton astutely concealed in the mane of the opposing horse. But it ruined Mose's reputation, and mayhap damaged his purse. He was set down as an *Hechicero* (sorcerer) by his Sonoranian antagonist and the second race fell through.

The first three American families permanently settled in the city, in 1850, were those of J. G. Nichols, J. S. Mallard, and Louis Granger. John Gregg, son of Mr. Nichols, was the first American boy born—April 15th, 1851. Among the novelties of a strange region, emigrants could not fail to notice the vivacity and robustness of the native-born children, and the large proportion of persons of an advanced age. April 24th, 1858, died at Santa Ana, Doña Guadalupe Romero, aged 115 years, leaving a son, in the city, upwards of 75 years. She came here in 1771, wife of a soldier named Moreno. Where Downey Block stands, we miss the time worn, little old gentleman who was wont to sit there all day before the humble adobe—cared for by two faithful daughters, after the mother had left the scene. A soldier of by-gone days, to judge from the antique dress which he delighted to wear; in the same he was buried, at the age of 92 years, July 29th, 1859. This was Don Antonio Valdez, who had served at San Diego, San Gabriel, and Santa Barbara, and in many an Indian chase or combat. The men appeared to fine advantage, in showy old style ranchero attire, on their gay and spirited horses. Of the·

ladies, few words might scarce reflect the true judgment of an *estrangero*, certes, it was admiration of elegance and naivete and kindness all with good sense and wit so happily blended, by some rare gift of Nature. That vener able religious pile on the plaza did not have pews. To see them kneeling in vari-colored silks of that time—and their *rebosas*—what gorgeous garden imaginable of dahlia and tulip of every hue could charm half so much ? Then a perpetual *baile*—but 1850 is gone, or fashions have changed, perhaps.

Of the one hundred and three proprietors of town-farms in 1848, before referred to, eight were foreigners: Abel Stearns, Louis Bouchet, Louis Vignes, Juan Domingo, Miguel N. Pryor, William Wolfskill, Louis Lemoreau, Joseph Snooks—an Englishman, a German, three French, three "Yankees"—so has the city ever been, cosmopolitan. Under the sound policy adopted at the beginning, for the disposition of pueblo lands, the natural course of business, and family changes, the proprietorship of real property is much altered. Those of Spanish origin, who number 3,000 souls within the city, and about an equal number outside in the county, retain good agricultural tracts. Within the patent of the city are 17,752 acres. The increase of culture of fruit trees—and ornamental too—is remarkable. In 1847, probably were set out two hundred young walnut trees; only three bearing are remembered—one on the east side of Don Louis Vignes' place, one larger in the middle of the Pryor Vineyard, another, very large, of Claudio Lopez. The almond was unknown. San Fernando and San Gabriel had a few olives. Long before 1840, the Californians had the fig, apricot, peach, pear, and quince. The County Surveyor's Report of January 1st, 1876, gives fruit trees as follows: Quince, 1,425; apricot, 2,600; fig, 3,600; pear, 5,800; apple, 8,590; peach, 14,200; olive, 2,170; English walnut, 6,000; plum, 300; there are also cherries. In 1856, there were 648 walnut trees. The value of the fruit crop of 1875 was $525,000. Plums were introduced by O. W. Childs. Seeds of the sweet almond, in 1855, were first planted by William Wolfskill, which were brought from the Mediterranean by H. F. Teschemaker, of San Francisco. Last January this county had 1,100 trees. Compared with the meagre agricultural crops from 1847 to 1855, the return for 1875 is: Beans, 24,400 bushels; onions, 28,350; buckwheat 1,350; rye, 11,760; wheat, 20,000; barley. 415,950; corn, 639,000; and a respectable showing of hops, tobacco, etc. Hay amounted to 10,250 tons. The enclosed land was 47,500 acres; total in cultivation 64,500 acres, of which 4,950 were in grape vines. Add, of honey, 571,230 pounds. O. W. Childs, in 1856, introduced bees. He paid $100, in San Francisco, for one hive and swarm. Afterwards, Sherman & Taylor brought here hives for sale. In 1850, there was one pepper tree, lofty and wide-branching, over the adobe house of an old lady living near the hills a short distance north of the plaza, the seeds of which came from a tree in the Court of the Mission of San Luis Rey. January 31st, 1861, John Temple planted a row in front of his Main street store. This the utilitarian woodman has not spared. But all the city is adorned with this graceful tree; and flowers of every name and clime—to rival an undying fragrance of the solitary Rose of Castile twenty years and more ago.

Of other trees that flourish now splendidly, William Rubottom, of Spadra, introduced pecans; William Wolfskill, persimmon; O. W. Childs, in 1856, black walnut—the seed from New York. About the same time H. P. Dorsey planted black walnut successfully at San Gabriel. In 1855, Solomon Lazard imported seeds of the Italian chestnut from Bourdeaux, France, which Wm. Woolfskill planted at his homestead, and afterward gave two of the trees to Heman C. Cardwell. These trees, now large and productive, may be seen at O. W. Childs' place. J. L. Sansevaine also brought chestnut seeds from France, about 1855.

As in older times, every full moon in 1850 the country was invaded by the Yutahs, under their famous chief, Walker, to steal horse stock. Expeditions sent after him were in general unsuccessful, now and then unfortunate: as happened in June, when he took off seventy odd of the best horses of Don Jose Maria Lugo, near the present Colton. One of the pursuing party was killed by him. Before that the New Mexicans of Agua Mansa had been a barrier to the incursions of these Indians, without always preventing them. In this year a volunteer company was raised by Gen. Bean, owing to hostile demónstrations by the Cahuillas of San Gorgonio. About June the "Irving party" of eleven men were killed by the Indians in the canada of Dona Maria Armenta. One only of the original twelve escaped, in the friendly shelter of some bushes. Juan Antonio, chief, had the boldness to offer fight to Bean. The rising of Antonio Garra, chief of Agua Caliente, in the fall of 1851, spread fear through Los Angeles of a general insurrection, from San Diego to Tulare. The danger soon passed away. The regulars and San Diego volunteers were under Captain George Fitzgerald. Gen. J. H. Bean commanded the Los Angeles volunteers; Myron Norton, Colonel and Chief of Staff; S. Bolivar Cox and B. S. Eaton, Corporals. Hon. H. C. Rolfe, Wm. Nordholdt—and many who are dead—were in service on the occasion. Estimable for many virtues, Gen. Bean met an untimely end, at San Gabriel, Sept. 9th, 1852. Our exposed position for a long time thereafter, in the Kern river and Mojave wars, and other troubles, kept amongst us officers of the U. S. army; and not seldom in active service. They possessed the regard of the people—Col. B. Beall, Majors Edward H. Fitzgerald and George R. Blake, Captains Davidson and Lovell, * * * General Winfield Scott Hancock, * * *. Lively recollections there are of the splendid band of the 2d Dragoons, Fort Tejon, that made more joyous the "Fourth of July, 1855," with General Banning as orator of the day; again, when Hon.Myron Norton, in 1857, stirred up patriotic feelings. The day had been kept from the beginning. Maj. Edward H. Fitzgerald lies in the Catholic Cemetery, Los Angeles. He died January 9th,1860, of consumption.

A quarter of a century, whereof reminiscences come involuntarily,is worthy of review. A record of crime must have attended this progress in manners and government. For one reason or another the people felt compelled often to "take the law into their own hands." Those moral tempests which agitated the community to its depths, slumber, we trust, to rise no more, in this better social condition.

For physicians, 1850 had Wm. B. Osborne, A. P. Hodges, W. W. Jones. A. W. Hope and Overstreet; in 1851, John Brinckerhoff, Thomas Foster and James P. McFarland; 1852, James B. Winston, and others. Dr. John S. Griffin returned to reside here in August, 1854. Dr. Richard S. Den was a physician esteemed highly, prior to 1843. Dr. Osborne was a native of New York,came to California in 1847,in Col. Stevenson's regiment. He put up the first drug store in 1850, which was followed by that of McFarland and Downey in 1851. Our first daguerreotypes were taken by him and Moses Searles, August 9th, 1851. He often acted as Deputy Sheriff—impossible to recount his various functions; a most useful man anywhere—friendly among his neighbors, of intelligence and public spirit. He was the projector of the famed artesian well near the hills on the west side of the city. It reached the depth of 780 feet, June 7th, 1856, but was abandoned by the company for want of funds. In 1852, fruit grafts had been introduced from New York by J. G. Nichols. In 1855 Dr. O. imported from Rochester a grand collection of roses and other choice shrubbery, as well as fruit trees. He was the first, too, in October, 1854, to ship fresh Los Angeles grapes, which were exhibited with admiration at a meeting of the business committee of the New York Agricultural Society at Albany. As late as November 17th, 1856, when Matthew Keller sent a like specimen, it was almost doubted at the U. S. Patent Office—"if such products are common in California." The third drug store war that of A. W. Hope, September, 1854; the fourth of Dr. Henry R. Myles, in 1860; then Winston & Welch—Dr. James C. Welch; then Dr. Theodore Wollweber, 1863. The first dentist was J. W. Gaylord. Dr. J. C. Welch died August 1st, 1869; he was a native of South Carolina. Dr. Hope was born in Virginia; died in the year 1855.

Let us make a diary of a year or two: 1851, May 24th, came news of the Stockton fire, on the 14th; loss over a million dollars. June 11th, Col. J. C. Fremont's visit created an agreeable sensation; 17th, died, Miss Rosa Coronel; 19th, feast of Corpus Christi was celebrated with great pomp; July 4th passed off with great enthusiasm; July 6th,Elder Parley P. Pratt held forth at the Court House; 19th, witnessed a performance of"The Rough and Ready Theatre," Herr Ritter, Manager, and the critic observes—"When Richmond was conquered and laid off for dead, (the spectators) gave the King a smile of decided approval." August 23d, Hon. Wm. M Gwinn, U. S. Senator was sojourning amongst us. September 1st, city lots sold at auction at from $20 to $31 each, purchaser to have choice. September 2d, died, Dona Maria Ignacia Amador, aged 91 years; 7th, Dona Felipa Dominguez, wife of Don Bernardo Yorba; 17th, Matilda Lanfranco, at 14; and 21st, at 88, Dona Ysabel Guirado. Oct. 5th, David W. Alexander started for Europe. Nov. 1st, Nicolas Blair, a Hungarian, married Miss Maria Jesus Bouchet. Nov. 8th was the first meeting of the Free and Accepted Masons at the Botica. The same day was published the marriage of Wm. J. Graves to Miss Soledad Pico at San Luis Obispo, on October 20th. Nov. 20th, at the Puente, aged 40 years, died Dona Incarnacion Martinez, wife of John Roland. Of her it is said truly, "Many will remember with what zeal she ministered to the weary traveler, with what care and anxiety she watched the sick bed—feeding the hungry and befriending the friendless. Her whole life was an exemplification of that enthusiasm in doing good which so particularly characterizes the christian woman." Dec. 14th were married Don Ignacio del Valle and Miss Ysabel Barrela. Dec. 22d, "Forefathers' Day," rejoiced thirty gentlemen by the presence of ladies and a supper at Monrow's with toasts, songs and speeches. Dec. 27th, 1851, Antonio Garra was executed at Chino by sentence of court martial, for insurrection November 23d, at Warner's rancho, and murder of American invalids Ridgley, Manning, Slack and Fiddler. Some of the property holders of this year were as follows, with the assessed value of personalty: Eulogio de Célis, 100,000 acres, $13,000; Jose Sepulveda, 102,000 acres, $83,000; John Temple, 20,000 acres, $79,000; Bernardo Yorba, 37,000 acres, $37,000; Antonio Maria Lugo, 29,000, $72,000; John Foster, 61,000 acres, $13,000; Abel Stearns, 14,000 acres, $99,000; Pio Pico, 22,000 acres, $21,000; John Roland, 29,000 acres, $70,000; Wm. Wolfskill, 1,100 acres, $10,000; Antonio Ignacio Abila, 19,000 acres, $14,000; Isaac Williams, $35,000; Ricardo Vejar, $34,000.

Through 1851 and a good while afterward the division of the State was a serious question. A common interest of money was five per cent. per month, often ten per cent.; a rate that commenced in 1848-'49, with the loans of John Temple to the hundreds eager to share in the *bonanza* at any sacrifice.

November 12, 1851, late of a bright moonlight evening, standing alone at the door of his office, Main street, (where is the "Oriental,") Benjamin Hayes was shot at by one within three feet on horseback. "The ball," says the Star, "passed through the rim of his hat and lodged in the wall on the the opposite side of the room, perforating in its progress the door, which is fully an inch in thickness. The assassins then instantly galloped off. A party of three, including the Sheriff, James R. Barton, tracked them about ten miles to a house; here they were received by five or six men on horseback, who charged upon them, fired several shots, and drove them from the ground. The Sheriff deemed it prudent to return to the city." He did so, obtained a posse, went back to the place of encounter, and made a search that proved ineffectual. It has always been believed that this assault was intended for another individual.

Eugene Hesse was the first Civil Engineer, followed in February 1852, by Vitus Wackenreuder, then by Henry Hancock, Adolph F. Waldemar, George Hansen, Frank Lecouvreur, William Moore, 1854, Ebenezer Hadley and W. W. Reynolds.

In 1852, January 7th, died Thomas S. Hereford, and 29th, of consumption, James W. Schureman, U. S. A. February 14, arrived Mrs. Emily M. G. Hayes, wife of Benj. Hayes, from Missouri, by way of New Orleans, Havana and Panama, in 43 travelling steamer days from St. Louis; March 6th, Nicolas Blair, tailor, had garden seeds for sale, fresh from Arroyo Seco, "superior to imported;" and subscription formed for a race course. March 13, death at age of 50 years, of Dr. George East. St. Patrick's Day kept up "till rather a late hour." March 27, marriage of Jose Maria Yndart to Miss Soledad Coronel. April 24, visit from Mr. Bartlett, Boundary Commissioner. July Fourth, English oration by Louis Granger, Spanish by Don Clemente Rojo: with 100 guns, a barbecue and ball at 'Don Abel's.' August 21, Don Antonio F. Coronel was County Superintendent of Common Schools. On the same day the first rumor arrived of the death of Henry Clay at Washington, on June 30th (he was born in 1777). Aug. 27th, Land Commissioners came. At the September election the total vote of the city was 386; total population of the county then, according to the census, probably unreliable, was, whites, 4,093; Indians, 3,693, foreign, 295; total, 7,831. The vote of the city of Los Angeles, September, 1875, was 2,549. Sept. 23d, grand ball at the dwelling of Don Manuel Garfias, in honor of the Land Commissioners. Sept. 16th, Col. J. Bankhead Magruder, U. S. A., and Andrew B. Gray, late of the U. S. and Mexican Boundary Commission, were in the city. Sept. 26th, death of Nicolas Blair, aged 30 years, an amiable, popular, enterprising man. October 2d, Sea Bird promises to make three trips monthly; freight on downward trip $20 per ton (now $5 per ton). Oct. 31, Rev. James G. Johnson, Cumberland Presbyterian, preached at the Court House—present city hall. November 1st, first political procession (Pierce), under Nordholdt, Lecke, Goller—transparencies and the Padre's little brass cannon—attempting to fire it off, "George the Baker" was badly burned. Nov. 13th, Nordholdt and Goller set up the grand Panoramic Exhibition of Windsor Castle, St. Peter's Church and Vatican, Jung Frau, Berlin, Vienna, Amsterdam. Nor had the "bull-fights" been missing at the "Feast of our Lady." Nov. 27th, first news published of the death of Daniel Webster, which had taken place on Oct. 24th. He was born Jan. 18th, 1782. Dec. 12th, the Spanish troupe played a drama of "The Immortal Poet, Don Jose Zorillo." Besides the Bella Union, the city through the year had boasted minor hotels—in March, The American, Harry Munrow; in May, Sportsmen's Hall, H. Malcolm; September, "Arkansas," at the noted corner. This was the harvest year of Joaquin Murietta, who kept the county in terror; however, he did not kill any one. On New Years' day, 1852, the county owed $47,017; and the State, $2,349,483. At the general election for Governor, Sept. 1855, Los Angeles county polled 1,479 votes; in 1875 the vote was 5,175. Peter Biggs was the first barber. As a slave, he was sold to an officer at Fort Leavenworth. At the close of the war, left on California territory, his freedom was necessarily recognized. He lived here many years thereafter. In the Spring of 1850, probably three or four colored persons were in this city. In 1875 they number about one hundred and seventy-five souls; many of whom hold good city property, acquired by their industry. They are farmers, mechanics, or of some one or other useful occupation; and remarkable for good habits. They count some seventy-five voters. Robert Owen, familiarly by Americans called "Uncle Bob," came from Texas in December, 1853, with "Aunt Winnie," his wife, two daughters, and son, Charley Owen. They survive him. He was a shrewd man of business, energetic, and honorable in his dealings; made money by Government contracts and general trade. He died, well esteemed by white and colored, August 18th, 1865, aged 59 years. Of the society of Mexican Veterans are five colored men: George Smith, George Diggs, Lewis G. Green, Paul Rushmore and Peter Byus. The last named was born in Henrico county, Va., in 1810, and served with Col. Jack Hayes, Gen. Z. Taylor, and Capt. John Long. He was at the battle of Monterey. Rushmore was born 1829, in Georgia; served on Taylor's line. He drove through the team of Col. John Ward and James Douglass from Chihuahua to Los Angeles. Smith and Diggs, the first born in New York, the second in the District of Columbia, both served on the ship Columbus, Commodore Biddle and Capt. Selfridge. Green was born in North Carolina, 1827; was a seaman on the Portsmouth, Captain John B. Montgomery; and in the navy nine years and eight months, on the store ship Erie, Cyane, Constitution, Pennsylvania and Vermont.

In 1850 the Bella Union was the only hotel. This was the official residence of Gov. Pio Pico, at the taking of the city by Commodore Stockton, in August, 1846; and continued to be occupied by the United States, for soldiers' quarters, till May, 1849. It had come into the hands of Mr. B. D. Wilson. It served as a species of hotel until after the county organization, when it was rented for a Court House. October 4th, 1851, it was reopened by Gibson & Hodges, in opposition to the "Eagle Hotel," Bailey & Overstreet, which had been started January 3d. Winston & Hodges then conducted it awhile, and sold out, March 5th, 1853, to Dr. Obed Macey, of El Monte.

July 22d, 1854, it was in the hand of Ross & Crockett. April 7th, 1855, Robert S. Hereford was proprietor. April 19th, 1856, it was transferred to Flashner & Hammell. Considerable improvements were commenced in October, 1858, and finished May, 1859, at a cost of $22,000, by Flashner & Winston. Marcus Flashner died June 29th, 1859. In 1860, John King was proprietor; in 1861, J. B. Winston & Co.; from 1860 to 1873, Gustavus H. Matfield. John King died December 20th, 1871. Through this series of years it is deeply associated with the recollection of our citizens. It is now the St. Charles; under Messrs. Salari & Whitney. The United States was built on property belonging to Don Juan N. Padilla—a name that recalls one of the most tragic events of the war of 1846, in California. May 31st, 1856, Joseph Waivel was proprietor; then, successively, H. Stasford, Webber & Hass, Louis Mesmer, Adams & Grey, Mesmer & Bremmerman, Hammel & Bremmerman. Mr. Mesmer, owner, has converted it into a massive, elegant brick structure. June 1st, 1868, Hammel & Dencker took possession, under a lease, and still conduct it. The Pico House, of recent structure, stands upon the premises once owned by Don Jose Antonio Carrillo—in his day very distinguished among his countryman—a member of the Mexican Congress and Judge of the Departmental Supreme Court. It was then a commodious adobe dwelling, with a red tiled roof. The proprietors are Don Antonio Cuyas & Co., under a lease. The Lafayette covers the site of the residence of Don Eulogio de Celis, an estimable and wealthy gentleman, native of Spain, who had been long on this coast, and in 1850 had retired from commercial pursuits. September 11th, 1859, Eberhard & Koll were proprietors, and there is reason to believe not without very considerable profit. January 1st, 1862, the firm was composed of Frederick W. Koll, Henry Dockweiler, and C. Fluhr. This last gentleman became sole proprietor in 1864. The business is conducted by Fluhr & Gerson. This vast building has been entirely reconstructed within the past two years. Don Eulogio de Celis died at Bilbao, Spain, January 27th, 1869.

In the Spring of 1850, the resident population of the city scarcely exceeded twenty-five hundred; augmented by January, 1853, to about 3,000, including 300 from the United States, and among these a large proportion of families. In those days of disorder the peaceful slumbers of the citizens were guarded by the Voluntary Police, of one hundred men, under Dr. A. W. Hope, as Chief. Among the lieutenants, or privates, we recognize, July, 1851, Messrs. Alexander, Olvera, S. C. Foster, Ogier, Brent, Joseph Yancey, Wheeler, J. G. Downey, Nichols, F. L. Guirado, Juan Sepulveda, Keller, Hayes. Often later were the streets enlivened by the martial tread of the military companies required, from time to time, in our wild circumstances. The 22d day of February, 1855, was celebrated by the City Guards, Captain W. W. Twist, and their first anniversary ball given in May. Ringgold's Light Artillery organized June 7th, of that year. The Los Angeles Rangers was older. The Legislature of 1854 appropriated $4,000 for their equipment; they celebrated their first anniversary August 6th, of that year. They had proved always efficient. March 26th, 1857, a rifle company was formed, under Captain Twist; and May 9th, the French infantry corps, 105 strong, Captain C. A. Faralle. The Rifleros de Los Angeles, Pantaleon Zavaleta, Captain, were established March, 1873; the Los Angeles Guard, September 8th, 1874—Captain, James Bartlett; First Lieutenant, Thomas Bowlin; Second Lieutenant, Charles Hagan.

We crave a thought for all who, in art or literature, have adorned this home of their choice. Friendship has a tear for some. Edward J. C Kewen, in 1860, charmed by his eloquence. Ina (Colbraith) was here then. Mrs. Caroline Hartman has left memorials of her taste in painting (portraits of Don Santiago Arguello, General John A. Sutter),and of ours(often she sweetly treats of California) was the fame of her writings in Atlantic periodicals. Mrs. Hartman died February 28th, 1861.

*   *   *   *   *   *   *   *

An important step toward public improvement was the establishment of the "Star," May 17th, 1851, a newspaper that has always exercised a salutary influence. The first number appeared of that date, with John A. Lewis and John McElroy, publishers; subscription, $10 per annum; in English and

Spanish. In July, Wm. H. Rand became associated with those gentlemen, as the firm of Lewis, McElroy, and Rand. November 4th, McElroy sold out to Lewis & Rand. October 19th, 1854, McElroy again became interested; the business to be hereafter conducted by J. S. Waite & Co. It was then Democratic in politics. December 15th, 1855, J. S. Waite was sole publisher and proprietor. By this time its Spanish advertisements had been transferred to the "Clamor Publico." April 12th, 1856, Waite sold to William A. Wallace, who, on June 7th following, sold to Henry Hamilton. Before this time the "Star" had given to light the letters of Hugh Reid, upon the Los Angeles Indians; some good original poems, in Spanish, of Don Manuel Clemente Rojo; had republished the life of Father Junipero Serra, founder of California civilization; and in a thousand ways had brought out full information upon the resources of this section. It was most ably conducted by Mr. Hamilton, through a trying period. Mr. Wallace deserves mention also for his contributions to the botany, especially of this county, through the year 1854, when he had means and leisure for explorations. James S. Waite is a well-to-do farmer in Santa Cruz. Henry Hamilton reposes at his olive garden of San Gabriel Mission—place of beauty which "Shenstone may have envied."

The "Clamor Publico," wholly in Spanish, was well edited, by Don Francisco P. Ramirez, from its birth, June 19th, 1855, until its death, December 31st, 1859. Don Pancho was born in this city. In 1860, 1861, and part of 1862, he was State Printer and editor of Official Journal of the State of Sonora. He returned here in 1862, and during part of that year and in 1863 he was Register of the U. S. Land Office, Los Angeles. From 1864 to 1868, he was one of the editors of "El Voz del Nuevo Mundo," San Francisco; and in 1865 State Translator for California, in the Spanish language. Awhile he was connected with "La Cronica," Los Angeles, whose publication was begun May 4th, 1872, E. F. Teodoli & Co., proprietors; writers, Don Eulogio F. de Celis and brothers. For the past three years or more he has devoted himself to the practice of law.

July 20th, 1854, appeared the "Southern Californian," published by Butts, Richards & Co., Wm. Butts editor. October 31st, 1855, the editors were William Butts and John O. Wheeler; November 10th it was suspended; January, 9th, 1856, John P. Prodic was the publisher. It contained essays in Spanish, by Don Juan Bandini, on the Land Question. Its press and materials were transferred to publish the "Southern Vineyard," the first number of which appeared March 20th, 1858, by John J. Warner; becoming semi-weekly December 10th of that year, and closing June 8th, 1860. Both offices, and that also of the "Clamor Publico," were merged in the "Los Angeles News." In 1865, Conway sold his interest to A. J. King. It was then conducted by King & Waite; in 1868, Waite sold to R. H. Offat, when the firm became King & Offat, who continued it for a year. Waite then entered again. January, 1872, Charles E. Beane bought out the whole interest of King, and it was conducted under Beane, Waite & Co. In the Fall of that year Beane succeeded to the whole interest. December 1st, its publication was finally discontinued, and materials, etc., transferred to the MIRROR. From 1854 to 1860, Alonzo Waite had been a printer in the Star office. It is believed that some of the ablest pens—among them that of Colonel James G. Howard—are recognized in the News, particularly in articles affecting the material interests of this county.

In societies for benevolence, or social and personal improvement, Los Angeles has always abounded. Los Angeles Lodge, No. 42, F∴ and A∴ M∴, worked under dispensation from December 17th, 1853, and was chartered May 6th, 1854. Its first officers were: Master, H. P. Dorsey; Senior Warden, J. Elias; Junior Warden, Thos. Foster; Treasurer, J. R. Barton; Secretary, Timothy Foster; Senior Deacon, J. Rich; Tyler, W. A. Smith. Los Angeles Lodge, No. 35, I. O. O. F., was instituted March 29th, 1855, by General Ezra Drown. Its charter members were: E. Drown, L. C. Goodwin, Alexander Crabb, Morris L. Goodman, William O. Ard'nger, M. M. Davis, E. Wilson High.

The Hebrew Benevolent Society of Los Angeles was organized in the year 1854. Its President is Samuel Meyer; Secretary, L. Leon. The French

Benevolent Society (now President, F. V. C. de Mondran), bears date of March 1st, 1860. October 29th, 1859, the vice-consular flag of France was raised in this city by the estimable vice-consul, Mr. Jacob A. Moerenhout, amid the firing of cannon and fervid congratulations of his own countrymen, participated in by many other citizens. The last estimate of the French in this city made about 600 men, of whom one-half are believed to be married; with their families there might be two thousand. M. Moerenhout was born at Antwerp, Belgium, March 6th, 1797. He was appointed Consul of France to the Mexican Government at Monterey in the year 1845, and arrived at that city on a French man-of-war in 1846. Although that Consulate was suspended in 1848, he remained there in the discharge of its functions until 1850, when he went to France. In 1852 he returned to Monterey with the title of consul *honoraire* and as vice-Consul of France; he remained there until 1859, when he was appointed in the same capacity to the city of Los Angeles. The Teutonia-concordia was formed December 31st, 1859, with thirty-eight members: President, C. H. Classen; Vice-President, H. Hammel; Secretary, H. Hensche; Treasurer, Lorenzo Leck. It held its anniversaries and no doubt was joyous, as Germans always are; but ultimately merged itself in the Turnverein Germania June 19, 1871. President now. George Reinecker; Vice-President, B. Marxen; Treasurer, C. Brode; Secretary, Henry Glass. The Germans with their wives and children are not less than two thousand. The Irish, including their families, are over one thousand in this city and county. They have a branch of the Ancient Order of Hibernians, which has about a hundred members; instituted here August 16th, 1875, with officers as follows: County Delegate, Daniel Douherty; President Martin Golden; Vice-President, B. J. Flynn; Financial Secretary, Peter Lunny; Recording Secretary, William Farley; Treasurer, Richard Malony. Its officers remain the same except President, who is Daniel Mc Carthy, and Martin Golden succeeds Mr. Flynn as Vice President. There are Temperance and other societies for benevolent objects, of recent dates, Order of Red Men, Knights of Pythias, etc.

The Merrill Lodge No. 299, I. O. G. T., was organized December 28th, 1867. Its officers are, July 4th, 1876: Jesse Yarnell, W. C. T.,Marion Caystile, W. V. T., Del. Condit, W. R. H. S., Mary Whitehorn, W. L. H. S., Wm. L. Todd, W. S., Ed. Stump, W. A. S., F. A. Gibson, W. F. S., J. R. Brierly, W. T., C. Stamps, W. M., Katie Caystile, W. D. M., T. J. Caystile, W. I. G., P. W. Dooner, W. O. G., J. J. Ayers, P. W. C. T., Tom B. Wade, W. C. The Catholic Abstinence Society has as President Patrick Connelly; Vice President, John P. Moran, jr.; Secretary, David Weldt; Chaplain, Rev. Peter Verdaguer. At an earlier day were Sons of Temperance and other organizations maintained with considerable enthusiasm. The Mechanics' Institute belonged to the years 1858-'60, before which, Dr. Thomas J. White, J. R. Scott, Esq., and other gentlemen, delivered able lectures. July 1st, 1859, the doors of the Library Association were opened to the public. An Agricultural Society was matured in December, 1859. The Spanish-American Benevolent Society came June 1st, 1875, D. Garcia President; preceded in 1863 by the Jurez Political Club, L. Benavides now President.

The first hospital, "The Los Angeles Infirmary," for the sick, was opened May 31st, 1858, in the house of Don Cristobal Aguilar, by the Sisters of Charity. These ladies emigrated from their mother house, St. Joseph's, Emmetsburg, Md., and settled at Los Angeles in the year 1855. Subsequently they have erected an extensive hospital of brick, with garden and orchard surrounding it, in the upper part of the city.

Contrary to what has been said sometimes, the native Californians were never indifferent to the education of their children, as the acts of the Departmental Assembly and Ayuntamientos prove, by constant efforts from the time of Governor Figueroa and before. It must be borne in mind their their local councils had not faculty to impose a property tax for any purpose, and their annual revenue seldom exceeded one thousand dollars. We very day meet on the street a member of the Ayuntamiento of 1846, Don Luis Jordan, who on January 21st of that year, urging a plan for a primary school, uttered the noble sentiment: "Humanity, family ties, and the obligation of our office in mute voices tell us that we must not be indifferent to the helplessness of youth, lest to-morrow our neglect may bring down upon our own heads odium and execration."

We have before referred to certain measures of the Mexican Supreme Government in 1833-'34 to extend education in California, and to the school of Don Ignacio Coronel at Los Angeles. The first proposition for a college was from Rev. Antonio Jimenes, May 18th, 1850, in his application for a grant of town land to that end. About the same time, Rev. Dr. Wicks, Presbyterian, seconded by J. G. Nichols, opened the pioneer English school. As late as January, 1853, we had but four small schools, two of them teaching English. The oldest Public School houses are one on Bath street, the other on Spring street: both built under the trustees J. G. Nichols and John O. Wheeler. At San Gabriel, J. F. Burns and Cæsar C. Twitchel were teachers in 1854. Dr. John S. Griffin, June 7th, 1856, was elected Superintendent of Common Schools, with Francis Mellus, Agustin Olvera and Wm. A. Wallace as School Commissioners. Wm. McKee and Mrs. Thomas Foster taught for some time. Mrs. Hoyt had a school March 7th, 1857, and her daughter, Miss Mary E. Hoyt, November 26th, 1859—these ladies much honored and successful teachers; and also, Miss Anna McArthur. Among the ladies teaching at different epochs since 1860, were Miss Eliza Madigan, Hattie Scott. Frankie Scott, Maggie Hamilton, Eula P. Bixby, Emma L. Hawks, Clara M. Jones, E. Bengough; Messrs. H. A. Saxe and C. H. Kimball, Dr. T. H. Rose and Dr. W. T. Lucky bring up this fair record to the present hour. July 4th, 1875, Los Angeles county had near 8.000 children, according to the school census; school districts, 48; teachers, 72; Public School houses, 59; to be understood as including grammar, intermediate and primary schools.

The Institute and Orphan Asylum of the Sisters of Charity had commenced January 5th, 1856. St. Vincent's Catholic College for boys, after two years on the Plaza, was firmly established in 1857, in their present edifice. Its President is Rev. Michael Flynn.

Educational systems have been extended and brought nearer perfection within the past seven years. To those patient laborers of our earlier days—in adverse circumstances, often their best recompense was the consciousness of duty well done—society is grateful for the noble gifts of useful men and women whom it owes to their knowledge and faithful care.

The Israelites have always observed their festivals of the Old Law, by closing houses of business and meeting for worship at designated places. They number six hundred souls.

The first Methodist sermon was preached June, 1850, by Rev. J. W. Brier, at the adobe residence of J. G. Nichols, where the Court House now stands. Mr. Brier was an emigrant of 1849, on the Salt Lake route. At Death Valley, on the Desert, he had to put his wife and two children on an ox, himself afoot, and so entered Los Angeles. In 1853, Rev. Adam Bland was sent by the California Conference to this, "the Southern California Mission." He came "with his wife and little white-haired girl," found inadequate accommodations for his family, and a solitary member, who then lived out of town, Mr. J. W. Potts (still living here). Later in the year Mr P. came to reside in the city; and he and Rev. Mr. Bland constituted the whole membership "at quarterly meeting, and official meeting; except when Dr. M. Whisler and family might come in from "El Monte." This society now numbers 260 members. Rev. J. McHenry Calwell was minister here in 1854, and must have been in part of 1855, for in April of that year preaching is advertised for the Court House (present City Hall) signed by him; preachers, Rev. Adam Bland and Rev. R. P. Dunlop, the latter preacher at El Monte, the former Presiding Elder in 1854. At Los Angeles the successive preachers thereafter were, in 1855, Rev. N. R. Peck; 1856, Rev. Elijah Merchant; 1857, Rev. David Tuthill; 1866, Rev. C. Gillett; 1867, Rev. A. P. Hernden; 1868, Rev. A. Coplin; 1869 and '70, Rev. A. M. Hough; 1871, Rev. P. Y. Cool; 1872, Rev. S. H. Stump; 1873, Rev. J. W. Campbell; now Rev. Geo. S. Hickey, A. M. It will presently appear that Mr. Tuthill must have been here in 1859. Rev. Mr. Merchant died in 1856, at the "little parsonage on First street." For some of these facts we are indebted to the Methodist Church Record, kept in this city. The Methodists have church edifices at Santa Monica, Compton and Orange, and propose others at Florence and Lower Santa Ana. Their pastors are: Rev. M. M. Bovard, A. B., Compton; Rev. J. D. Crum, Santa Monica; Rev. J. M. Campbell, Orange and Anaheim; Rev. C. Shelling, Florence and Indiana Colony; Rev. I. N. Leiby, Westminster and Artesia; Rev. Adam Bland, Santa Ana and Tustin.

To go back a little: Rev. James Woods, Presbyterian, and Rev. James G. Johnson were among the earliest preachers. Rev. J. W. Ellis died at El Monte, February 29th, 1856. In August following, Rev. I. N. Davis left, for want of support. Los Angeles then was without any Protestant misister. As late as May, 1857, there was no Episcopal pastor. On that day, Dr. Matthew Carter announces himself as a lay reader, authorized only to administer burial rites. Rev. Elias Birdsall staid here a year, from the Spring of 1865, about which time Bishop Wm. Ingraham Kip made his first visit. Rev. Henry Hayes Messenger came to this city July 19th, 1866. He had been a missionary on the west coast of Africa, near Cape Palmas, from 1858 to 1862. His health impaired, he returned to Ohio; after four years, concluded to try California. He lives at Orange, in this county, sometimes preaching, but a good deal devoted to horticultural pursuits, especially the banana, pine-apple and other tropical plants. After Mr. Messenger, came Rev. J. B. Gray, Rev. J. J. Talbot, Rev. Robert Burton, and now Rev. William II. Hill. At Anaheim, is Rev. J. M. Hubbard, Episcopal. In 1859, El Monte had Rev. R. C. Fryer and Rev. John A. Freeman. On May 4th, of the same year, an organization was formed by Rev. Wm. E. Bourdman (the author), under the title of the First Protestant Society, with a Constitution declaring that its members "unite for the purpose of supporting Protestant worship here;" signed by Isaac S. K. Ogier, Wm. McKee, A. J. King, C. Sims, Charles S. Adams, Wm. S. Morrow, D. McLaren, Thos. Foster, Wm. II. Shore, N. A. Potter. The corner-stone of St. Athanasius Church—that on the hillside below the High School—was laid in 1864. The following ladies constituted its choir: Mrs. Caroline Hartman, Mrs. Nancy Wheeler, Mrs. Gen. W. S. Hancock, Mrs. Major S. P. Hentzelman, Mrs. G. W. Mix, Mrs. Adeline E. Morgan, who is now in Florida, and widow of Mr. Osias Morgan, Miss Mary E. Hoyt, Mrs. Julia Wheeler, Miss Maria Schotchler, who married Mr. II. N. Alexander, and died soon afterward, Mrs. W. E. Boardman and niece, Miss Abbie Green. The lot was conveyed, by Francis Mellus, for the first Protestant Church that might be built, of which the Presbyterians availing themselves built this edifice, and transferred it to the Episcopalians. It was built under the direction of Rev. Mr Boardman. The Baptists have a church at Downey City. The present Congregationalist Church on New High street was built by Rev. Alexander Parker; he was follow by Rev. J. T. Wills; the minister now is Rev. D. T. Packard. The Presbyterians have Rev. Dr. A. F. White.

Rev. Dr. Pierce and Rev. T C. Barton officiated here before 1859, and in that year Rev. W. E. Boardman, Presbyterian, Rev. D. Tuthill, M. E., and Rev. Mr. Newton, M. E. South. Referring to the three gentlemen last named as being located here October 22, 1859, the Star says: "With this force of pious and talented clergymen, we have no doubt the spiritual interest of the various Protestant denominations will be duly attended to. We did not mention, in the foregoing, the Reverend Dean and clergy of the Catholic Church, because every one knows they are the pastors of the Church of the great mass of our citizens,—indeed, the founders of our city itself; and that the doors of the Church stand open for divine service all day and nearly all hours."

Rt. Rev. Thaddeus Amat, of Barcelona, Spain, was consecrated Bishop of Monterey in 1854. In 1859 he received the title of Bishop of Monterey and Los Angeles, and established his See in this city. Rev. Blas Raho had preceded him in 1856, as parish Priest, at whose death Rev. Francis Mora came, in 1863, as Rector of the Cathedral and Vicar General. August 3d, 1873, Rev. Francis Mora was consecrated Bishop Co-adjutor. Rev. Peter Verdaguer is Parish Priest, Rev. Miguel Duran, Assistant. The Catholic Church on the Plaza was built in the year 1821; a new roof put on in 1841

4

by Rev. Fr. Sanchez. It was improved to its present state by Rev. B. Raho. The Cathedral on Main street, which is the largest Church edifice perhaps in this State, was commenced May 1st, 1871, and consecrated April 30th, 1876. At Santa Ana (of the Yorbas) is a Church built at the expense of Don Bernardo Yorba, many years ago. In August, 1869, Rev. Peter Verdaguer, then pastor of San Gabriel built a Church at Anaheim, upon a lot granted to him on condition of improvement. Its pastor is Rev. Victor Fouron. Small tracts belong to the Catholic Church at each of the old Missions of San Fernando, San Gabriel and San Juan Capistrano, acquired by confirmation of the U. S. Courts. The grazing lands surrounding those places were in general granted by the Mexican Government to private individuals,—as at San Fernando, 121,619 acres to Don Eulogio de Celis; at San Juan, various fine ranchos to John Foster. San Fernando has no Priest; its Church is out of repair. Famed in 1854 for its olives, it is now the cynosure of all railway expectations. The first through train from San Fernando to Spadra bears date April 15th, 1874. The great tunnel of the Southern Pacific Company was commenced in April, 1875; its completion is predicted confidently by Superintendent E. E. Hewitt on September 20th, 1876. The Spadra trunk passes alongside of the weather-beaten adobe walls of San Gabriel. A new and solid roof was put upon its Church in 1863, by Rev. Cipriano Rubiou. Its present pastors are Rev. Joaquin Bot and Rev. Hugh McNamee. Its bells, celebrated in song for their sweet tones, date far back into the last century. The Priest of San Juan Capistrano is Rev. Joseph Mut. Since the earthquake of 1812, divine service has always been held in a large room fronting on the Court. An effort was made some years ago to repair the old Church, which failed for want of means. When Commodore Stockton passed, January 5th, 1846, it is described as "evidently once a handsome building; well finished with cut stone arches over the doors, windows, etc.; the cornice of the same; the rest of the building of stone, covered with cement and stucco work. Many families then were at the Mission, and Mr. John Foster resided there. Extensive dams were standing that had been used for irrigation, and the valley appeared to have been formerly kept in a high state of cultivation. The Church is now, or has been, used for a stable."

Don Juan Foster began to occupy this place in the year 1844, and remained there until he took possession, in 1864, of his princely estate of Santa Margarita. He became so identified with it, that he used to be saluted "San Juan Capistrano" as often as by his family appellation. Nevertheless, not to him does it owe its name, but to a personage who was born at the town of Capistrano, near the city of Aquila, in the kingdom of Naples. In a work which treats of these subjects very learnedly, it is stated as follows: "This zealous defender of the Christian religion was son of a French knight, who married in Italy while attached to the retinue of the Duke d'Anjou, who, at Avignon, had been crowned King of Naples. After study of civil and canonical law, he was made a Judge at Perusa, and was distinguished by brilliant talents and eloquence. He married there, but on the death of his wife he entered into the religious order of Franciscans (by whom the California Missions were all established). His custom was to eat once a day, and for thirty-six years he did not taste of meat—sleeping but three hours at night on the floor of his cell. He was eminent in the pulpit. He filled many employments under Papal appointment in Germany, Hungary, Bohemia, Poland, and elsewhere. Mahomet II, the terror of Europe, took Constantinople in the year 1453; now master of twelve kingdoms and more than two hundred cities, he besieged Belgrade, in 1456. San Juan Capistrano was by the Pope appointed preacher and leader of the Crusade. Hungarian, Transylvanian and Russian combined, San Juan in front, crucifix in hand, met Mahomet. At the first onset the Ottoman army was routed, Mahomet wounded-and his troops cut to pieces—a victory which the Princes all ascribed to the zeal and prayers of San Juan. He died the same year in Hungary at the age of 71 years. In 1690 he was solemnly canonized by Pope Alexander VIII." We have already explained the Pueblo name, as distinguished from that of the Mission. This pretty sea-side valley has had a various history. Its aborigines were remarkable from the first, according to the account left of them in the biography of Father Junipero Serra, for their gentleness of disposition:

and ever since have been noticed for their comely appearance and good qualities. In 1862-63 the small-pox nearly exterminated them. The pirate Bouchard held high wassail three nights and days within its sacred walls, his outlaw crew, wild from its well-filled cellars, Priests and neophytes meanwhile sheltered by the woods of Trabuco.' About 1859, Daniel Sexton had weary digging under one of its rooms for hidden treasure, until the condescending proprietor feared to see his house tumbling down over his head. Ships for trade had anchored in its snug bight, and its hot spring, twelve miles distant, invited invalids to healing waters. Beyond doubt it was a regularly organized Mexican pueblo, yet by sleepy neglect missed a confirmatory decree, and the homes of the too confiding inhabitants may have been the prey of speculators. November 11th, 1875, its land was finally entered as a town site, amounting to 567.07 acres, for $708.89; the only town site that has been entered in the U. S. Los Angeles District. In more prosperous days, was there ever a gayer people? And where a firmer fortitude in adversity? Primitive simplicity sought to keep the reign at San Juan. Seldom they elected a "Justice of the Peace;" nor often had they a dispute which "Don Juan"—whether Foster or Abila—could not lull and compose. So in quiet lived Santiago Rios, Brigido Morrillo, Pedro Verdugo, Matias Olivares, Blas Aguilar, Hermenegildo Bermudez, children, grand children —and friends—at sixty miles from Los Angeles, and seventy other wearier miles from San Diego—too far for excitement or news, unless when the politician irrepressible might stray within their fold, or a charmed visitor share the cheerful board.

On January 22d, 1857, came the band of Pancho Daniel and Juan Flores. Through the day they plundered the stores of Miguel Krazewsky, Henry Charles, and Manuel Garcia, finishing their work by cruel murder of the German merchant, George W. Pflugardt. This led to events which we may briefly relate. Having received some previous information of movements of these robbers, Sheriff James R. Barton, on the night of the 22d, left this city with a party consisting of Wm. H. Little, Charles K. Baker, Charles F. Daley, Alfred Hardy and Frank Alexander. Within fifteen miles of San Juan, on the San Joaquin rancho, next morning, Little and Baker advanced a few hundred yards in pursuit of a man in view on horseback. The bandits sallied out from behind a hillock, eight in number, instantly killed Little and Baker, then attacked Barton and companions. After a short conflict Barton was killed, and Daley pursued with like fate. The other two, by the fleetness of their horses escaped and brought this sad intelligence to Los Angeles. Words cannot picture the horror and grief that filled all men. Revenge became instantly the sole thought. Five companies, French, Germans, and Americans, were at once organized, and two besides of native Californians; one also at El Monte, one at San Bernardino. A company of U. S. Infantry came from Fort Tejon under Lieutenants Magruder and Pender. At San Diego an express had brought information of the death of Pflugardt. Under a warrant issued by the District Judge, Captain H. S. Burton placed at the disposal of Sheriff Joseph Reiner thirty of his artillerymen, mounted, under Lieut. Mercer, who proceeded to San Juan. The Los Angeles companies scoured the country, and some of the bandits were taken and hung. A company under James Thompson was sent towards Tujunga. Some of the U. S. Infantry with him were stationed on the look-out at Semi Pass. Two of the soldiers, hid behind the rocks, succeeded in arresting a man who had come there for water. He was without arms, mounted on a poor horse, and had a little dried beef on the saddle behind him. He said his name was Juan Gonzales Sanchez; that he belonged to and had come from San Fernando Mission; was out hunting horses, and would go no further. Taken into camp, he was recognized by Don Pancho Johnson as Juan Flores. In the presence of almost the entire population, near the top of Fort Hill, he was executed Feb. 14th, 1857, in accordance with a vote of the mass of the people. James R. Barton was of Howard county, Mo.; emigrated to Mexico in 1841; came to California in 1843. William Hale Little was reared in Texas, near Palestine, Anderson county; aged 33 years. Charles K. Baker was born at Rock Spring, De Soto county, Mississippi; aged 26 years: he was last from Sequin, Texas. Charles F. Daley was a native of New York; 30

years of age. Pancho Daniel was captured by Sheriff Murphy in January, 1858, concealed in a haystack in the vicinity of San Jose. He was put in jail in Los Angeles. His case came before the District Court,—Benj. Hayes, Judge—on March 15th, E. J. C. Kewen his counsel. He pleaded "not guilty" to the indictment for the murder of Charles K. Baker, Charles F. Daley and Pflugardt. Col. Kewen then retired from the case and K. H. Dimmick was appointed by the Court to conduct his defense. Various proceedings took place. It appearing impossible to get a jury out of a venire of ninety-six persons, the case was continued; C. Sims, Attorney for defendant. At the July term, from illness of C. Sims, C. E. Thom was assigned as associate counsel. A challenge to the whole panel of 96 jurors was sustained by the triers, and a further panel of 96 jurors ordered to be returned on August 9th. The Court then sustained a challenge for bias of the Coroner, and the case was continued until the next term. November 15th the Elisor was challenged for bias in summoning a panel of 96 jurors. This challenge was not sustained. A motion for a change of venue was then made, argued, and the case transferred to Santa Barbara county, in the Second Judicial District. General E. Drown was District Attorney. On November 30th, about 6½ o'clock in the morning, Richard Mitchell, the jailor, was on his way to market. He was stopped by six or eight persons, who demanded the keys of the jail, which he delivered after some hesitation. A piece of artillery was planted so as to bear upon the door of the jail, and a large number of men marched-from a neighboring corral The doors of the prison were opened and Pancho Daniel was summoned to leave his cell, which he did with coolness and resignation. At twenty minutes past 7 A. M. he was hung within the jail yard. The body was delivered to his wife for interment. A Coroner's Jury examined a number of witnesses and rendered a verdict that "he came to his death by being hanged by some persons to the jury unknown."

Freshets of the river have been exaggerated in the excitement of the moment. At Los Angeles, the flood of 1861-62 began with the rain on Christmas eve, 1861,and continued almost without intermission until January 17th, 1862, on which last day, 3 o'clock P. M., fell tremendous torrents of water, accompanied by loud claps of thunder and vivid lightning. Soon the little irrigating streams of the city flowed on as usual, and the traces of the storm were easily effaced. In fact they were but little more serious than that of Christmas day, 1860; or of November 29th 1859, which was acknowledged to have "accomplished miracles for the good of the country." For many years this of December-January, (1861-62) was the heaviest that had fallen. The city dam was damaged; some adobe houses fell; travel on the roads was considerably impeded; the South-east gales delayed the arrival of the Brother Jonathan at San Pedro. At El Monte the San Gabriel river made a new channel, entering near the town of Lexington; but the danger was soon averted by the energy of the inhabitants. On the Santa Ana, at Anaheim, the overflow was rather advantageous than otherwise, to the vineyards. Some thirty miles higher up, by accessions of torrents from the mountain creeks of San Bernardino, on the night of January 17th,the flood destroyed the thriving New Mexican settlement of Agua Mansa (Gentle Water). There was no loss of life, the sleeping inhabitants having timely alarm by the bells of their Church; but every former sign of culture was obliterated by the waste of sand which the rush of waters spread over the whole valley, and five hundred souls, houseless, were turned out upon the surrounding hills. These rains extended to the rivers San Diego and Mohave. On the banks of the first, at the town of San Diego, improvements had begun to be made, in forgetfulness of the experience of 1811 and 1825 and 1840. Boats brought off the women and children. The Mohave, which seldom reaches the Colorado, on January 20th had swollen that river, and Fort Yuma was an island. Not a drop of these rains had fallen at Fort Yuma, or on the Colorado Desert. For this fact we are indebted to Dr. Prentiss, Surgeon U. S. A. at Fort Carleton, and Lieut. Nichols, who left Fort Yuma January 20th and came to San Bernardino in four and a half days by San Gorgonio Pass. At Algodones, on the river Colorado, where Dr. P. encamped the first day, that river rose six feet during the night. Lieut. Nichols went one day forty-five miles without water. February 4th, at night, the Senator, Capt. Seely, encountered off

Point Concepcion the severest gale that he had ever experienced on this coast. The same day, at 10 o'clock A. M., at San Bernardino, a shock of earthquake was felt, lasting a second; oscillation from east to west.

No permanent injury has been done here, nor in California, by "earthquakes," since December 8th, 1812, when San Juan Capistrano and La Purissima Churches were destroyed. There were sensible shocks in July, 1855, April 14th, May 2d, and September 20th, 1856. The shock of Friday, January 9th, 1857, was at twenty-five minutes past eight o'clock in the morning.

On the 10th and 17th, and subsequently, accounts of the phenome arena published in the Star, from which we summarize these interesting facts. At Los Angeles, the morning was calm, cool and clear, the sun shining brightly. The earth's motion was very gentle at first, those sitting at table supposing some one was shaking it; gradually it increased in violence till every house, with all its contents, were seen to rock from side to side, as if about to topple over. There were three distinct shocks—the pause between them being perceptible only to those who have long lived in countries where earthquakes are more common than here. The duration of the oscillation was fully two minutes. The vibration from north to south. In half an hour after another shock occurred, much less violent; another within an hour from that, and during the day a number of slight vibrations. At five o'clock in the afternoon, a shock occurred almost as severe as the first, which was followed at intervals by slight motions till about eleven o'clock, when another heavy one occurred. During the night several other vibrations were felt. On Saturday there were several slight shocks, with one severe one about eleven o'clock at night. Sunday was quiet till about eleven o'clock at night, when a pretty strong vibration was felt, and thereafter at intervals during the night. Monday, many say they felt shocks through the day. After that day the earth remained quiet. Through this county it was felt variously, but most sensibly at Fort Tejon; also, in San Bernardino, San Diego, and Santa Barbara Counties; at Monterey, Santa Cruz, San Jose, Stockton, San Francisco, Sacramento, Marysville.

"The waters of the Mokelumne, below Benson's Ferry, then much swollen by the late rains, were turned for a time over the surrounding country, leaving its bed nearly bare, while trees were settled several feet into the ground, and limbs were broken from others by the violent motion."—*Sacramento Age.*

"The movement was undulating, from north to south, without damage either to persons or property."—*Sacramento Union.*

"In San Jose Valley, the only damage was the cutting off or reducing in volume the streams of several of our artesian wells. In some instances the water has entirely ceased to flow to the surface, and in others, the stream was for a time greatly increased, and then subsided to about its former size."—*San Jose Tribune.*

"In the Counties of Santa Cruz and Monterey, it was a pretty hard shock, yet no buildings were affected."—*Pacific Sentinel.*

"At San Francisco, all the accompaniments of a second-class earthquake were experienced."—*S. F. Herald.*

"At Santa Barbara several houses were injured, but no lives lost."

William Denton, Esq., describes the shock at the upper crossing of the Mohave River, fifty miles from San Bernardino. Commencing with a harsh, grating noise, the motion of the earth became very violent, and lasted between thirty or forty seconds; two motions, apparently, vertical and oscillating. With great difficulty he could keep his feet. At night, in camp, he experienced two more shocks—about nine and eleven o'clock—which were not severe; the wind very high at the time. The first shock, at the Mohave crossing, was immediately succeeded by an appalling noise. At Kern Lake, the water in the river was forced back, and rose over the banks about four feet. All information makes the force of the shock gradually less as it approached northward—from Fort Tejon.

At Fort Tejon it was more severe than in any other part of the State, and is thus described in a published letter to the Star, from Alonzo C. Wakeman, Quartermaster's Deputy, U. S. A., of date January 11th, 1857:

"The first shock took place about thirty minutes past six o'clock A. M., on Friday, January 9th, which was succeeded, at twenty minutes previous to nine o'clock A. M., by a terrific shock. The vibrations have continued, at intervals, up to the present time, say five o'clock P. M. The earth has opened in many places for a distance of twenty miles. Amongst the narrow escapes from falling buildings, is that of the lady of Captain R. W. Kirkham, Assistant Quartermaster, who is absent from the post on official duty; also, Lieut. Col. B. L. Beall, commanding the post, who had barely sufficient time to escape from his bed amidst the falling of plaster, the crashing of material, falling of chimneys, etc. The line of disruption seems to extend from southeast to northwest. Mr. David W. Alexander, in from San Emigdio Rancho, reports that the beds of many small streams have been enlarged, and now form almost rivers; and that immense numbers of fish have been thrown out of the lakes upon the dry land. On January 20th, another severe shock was felt, and vibrations had been of frequent occurrence meanwhile. The troops betook themselves to their tents. The buildings occupied by Lieut. Col. Beall, Major Blake, Major Grier, Lieutenants Ogle and Magruder, and others, were all cracked and variously injured, but not beyond easy repair, as was found out on cooler inspection."

Since 1857, there has been no shock in this section of the State that has attracted more than a slight notice from the inhabitants generally."

Certainly we have not violated the maxim—"hasten slowly." The Senator, Capt. Thomas Seeley, three times a month, and the overland stage three times a week, in the Summer of 1859, were god-sends to the public. At sea, we were glad to have parted with Ohio, Goliah, Sea Bird, and Southerner, although memory is true to the pleasant companionship of their Haleys and other officers. On land we hailed Wells, Fargo & Co., April 11, 1857, when "Buck"—A. W. Buchanan, Esq.—came down to establish a branch; and have pardoned Gregory's great Atlantic and Pacific Express, of 1851, and the mails —a month and nineteen days from the East. We welcomed Paul and Chapman June 4th, 1859, with their "regular line once a week"—San Diego— 130 miles. What a contrast: The present, with the stages of David Smith semi-monthly to Visalia, April, 1857, and this, when a little over two years before we had made the Tejon road, at a cost of $6,000. The same year we had three wind-mills in the county. January 7, 1856, Heman C. Cardwell had just introduced Hovey's seedling strawberries. Up to September, 1855, there were no bee-hives in the county. January 1st, 1876, there were 10,386 hives. Then, too, "the finest orchard in Southern California," said the Star, was that of Wm. M. Stockton, near San Gabriel Mission, in sight of Fairy Lake Vineyard. The first U. S. patent was issued in 1859 to Don Manuel Dominguez, for San Pedro rancho. We did not get the telegraph until the end of 1860. Travel had so far improved by December, 1861, that Cattick & Co's stages were able to "leave Los Angeles on Mondays and Thursdays, returning Tuesdays and Saturdays"—62 miles; daily we go to breakfast at Los Angeles, from San Bernardino, and back to its fountains and groves ere nightfall. In the full fruition of railway communication between the Atlantic and Pacific—with a promise from every "sign of the times" of new lines of travel between ocean and ocean over other sections of our country— we may not forget that the first earnest public announcement of such blessing emanated from a gentleman who was then and is a citizen of Los Angeles. John J. Warner, being on a visit to Connecticut (his native State), by request of friends, prepared a lecture on California. This was delivered before a society at Rochester, N. Y., and afterwards at Upper Middletown, Conn., in the latter part of the year 1840; and early in 1841, portions of the same were published in the New York Journal of Commerce. Mr. W. advanced and demonstrated the proposition that the trade of Europe and the Atlantic States of the Union, with China, could be carried across the continent more advantageously by rail than by a ship canal at Panama. To him, then, we give the meed of praise for the first suggestion of this great enterprise.

San Pedro was often lively in 1840—and had been so in Mission times —by the trading vessels engaged, with active competition, in the purchase of hides and tallow. Francis Mellus gives a list of those on this coast, August 22d of that year, thirteen in number, as follows: "Ships—California (Capt. Arthur), Alciope (Clapp), Monsoon (Vincent), Alert (Phelps); Barques—Index (Scott), Clara (Walters); Hermaphrodite brigs—Leonidas (Stevens), Ayacucha (Dare); Brigs—Juan Jose (Dunkin), Bolivar (Nye); Schooners—Fly (Wilson), California (Cooper), Nymph, formerly Norse (Fitch), and two more expected." From 1844 to 1849 the merchants at Los Angeles city were, John Temple, Abel Stearns, Charles W. Flugge—found dead September 1st, 1852, on the plains below this city—B. D. Wilson and Albert Packard (Wilson & Packard), and Alexander Bell. To these add, in 1849, Antonio Cota, Jose Antonio Menendez, from Spain; Juan Domingo, Netherlands; Jose Mascarel, of Marseilles, and John Behn, of Grand Dutchy Baden. The last named came in 1848. He quit business in the Fall of 1853, died December 6th, 1868. Madame Salandie is to be added to those of '49. She came on the same ship with Lorenzo Lecke from Pennsylvania in that year, started at once a little store, butcher shop, loaning money, and general speculation. Juan Domingo came to California in 1829, by way of Lima, married here, was quite noted, died December 20th, 1858.

The first steamer that ever visited San Pedro was the Goldhunter, in 1849—a side-wheel, which made the voyage from San Francisco to Mazatlan, touching at way ports. The next was the old Ohio. At San Pedro, from 1844 to 1849, Temple & Alexander—D. W. Alexander—had the only general store, and they carried on all the forwarding business. The first four-wheel vehicle in this county, except an old-fashioned Spanish carriage belonging to the Mission Priests, was a rockaway carriage which this firm bought of Capt. Kane, Major Graham's Quartermaster, in January, 1849, paying him $1,000 for the carriage and two American horses. It created a sensation like that of the first Wilmington railway car on the 26th day of October, 1868. Goods were forwarded to Los Angeles, twenty-four miles, in carts, each with two yoke of oxen, yoked by the horns. The regular train was of ten carts, like the California *carretas*. The body was the same, but they had spoked wheels tired, which were imported from Boston. Freight was $1.00 per hundred weight; now it is $1.00 per ton. This style of importation continued until after 1850. The first stage line was started by Alexanders & Banning in 1852; the next by that man of iron, J. J. Tomlinson, whose death was early for the public good, June 7th, 1867. In 1851, D. W. Alexander purchased at Sacramento ten heavy freight wagons that had been sent in from Salt Lake by Ben Holliday, and in 1853 a whole train, fourteen wagons and 168 mules, that had come through from Chihuahua, paying therefor $23,000. So ox-carts were supplanted.

Alexander & Mellus became a new firm, at Los Angeles City, in 1850, continuing until 1856. Wilson & Packard dissolved December, 1851. John Temple and Alexander Bell kept up their separate stores. Other merchants of 1850 were: Jacob Elias, Charles Ducommon, Samuel Arbuckle, Waldemar, O. W. Childs, and J. D. Hicks—Childs & Hicks; Charles Burroughs, who died May 30th, 1856; M. Michaels, H. Jacoby, of violin celebrity, and who went rich to Europe; Jordan, Jose Vicente Guerrero, Jose Maria Fuentes, Jose Baltazar, of Prussia, Rimpau, Fritze & Co., with Morris L. Goodwin, Clerk, John Behn and Frank Laumeistre, a German; afterward, in the same year, Behn & Lamitre, and Mattias Savichi. This estimable gentleman was of Dalmatia. He died June, 1852, at sea, bound from Saint Thomas to London, leaving two young sons, of whom Francisco Savichi survives, a prominent citizen of Los Angeles. George Walters also had commenced business in this year. He was born at New Orleans, April 22d, 1809. After trapping and trading adventures in the Rocky Mountains, at Fort Hall, and elsewhere, under Captain Wyatt, and teaming between Westport, Bent's Fort, and Santa Fe, at last, near the end of 1844, he left New Mexico, in company of Jim Beckwith, James Waters (of San Bernardino), and others, and made his home at Los Angeles; and was not long in becoming one of the Chino prisoners, with B. D. Wilson and Louis Roubidoux. He enjoys advancing age, in the possession of good property. Mr. Wilson was Indian Agent, for Southern California, in 1853; in the same year made his place on Alameda street, which he sold to the Sisters of Charity for their Institute; and in 1854 began to put into effect his plans for Lake Vineyard. He removed there in 1856. He was born at Nashville, Tennessee, in 1811— is still full of enterprise. Mr. Packard went to Santa Barbara, entered into the practice of law, with horticultural improvements; is well off. John O. Wheeler and Osias Morgan—Wheeler & Morgan, until September, 1852—began in September, 1849, with trading establishments at Rincon, San Luis Rey, Pala, Agua Caliente. In May, 1850, after John Glanton had been killed by the Indians, they put up a branch at Fort Yuma. They, in fact, succeeded Wilson & Packard, in their store, in August, 1850. Mr. Morgan died several years ago. Mr. Wheeler was Clerk of the U. S. District Court, of the Southern District of California, from 1861 until its discontinuance, in 1866; then Deputy Clerk of the Circuit Court; from 1870 to 1873, Chief Clerk of the California Indian Superintendency, Col. B. C. Whiting, Superintendent; Deputy Collector of U. S. Internal Revenue of Second Division, First District, comprising Los Angeles, San Bernardino and San Diego Counties, which office he resigned January 1st, 1876.

In 1851, '52, '53, appear Lazard, Arbuckle & Bauman, Lazard & Bauman, S. Lazard & Co., Lazard & Kremer; Douglass & Sanford, 1852; Childs, Hicks & Wadhams (O. W. Childs, horticulturist, since 1856); Thomas Brown & Prudent Beaudry; Myles & Hereford—Dr. Henry R. Myles; Bauman & Katz; Hoffman & Laubheim; P. Beaudry & Armand Lemaitre until December, 1852, then P. Beaudry & Co.: Thomas S. Hereford; J. S. Mallard. January, 1853, there were three large dry goods' stores, and ten or more smaller houses that also kept a general assortment. Half a dozen others sold groceries and provisions exclusively. The liquor shop—its name was "legion." John Schumacher was here in 1848, one of Colonel Stevenson's regiment; went to the mines; returned in the Spring of 1853; put up a grocery and provision store. He is of Wirtemberg. In the same year he introduced *lager bier*, from San Francisco. It was not manufactured at Los Angeles until Christopher Kuhn, of Wirtemberg, established a brewery, in the latter part of 1854. John Kays was a good baker, 1847; John Behn afterward, awhile. Confectionery was made in 1850, by Papier; Joseph Lelong followed with the Jenny Lind Bakery, February 14th, 1851. French bread was used altogether, until August Ulyard commenced his bakery, in 1853. Lorenzo Lecke arrived November 5th, 1849. He was born in Denmark, February 25th, 1810; bought out John Behn, commenced a store in 1854, and perseveres in trade at the age of 66. The merchants of 1853, besides those already mentioned, were Joseph Newmark, Jacob Rich, and J. P. Newmark—Rich & Newmark; John Jones, who was the first wholesale liquor dealer, at the corner of Main and Commercial streets—Polaski & Goodwin's now; Jacob Morris, J. L. Morris and Morritz Morris—Morris Bros.; Felix Bachman, Philip Sichel and Samuel Laubheim—Bachman & Co.; Harris Newmark and E. Loewenthal—Newmark & Loewenthal; H. K. S. Labatt; Samuel Meyer and Loewenstein—Hilliard & Meyer; M. Norton and E. Greenbaum—Norton & Greenbaum; H. Goldberg, I Cohen, July 8th; Charles R. Johnson and Horace S. Allanson—Johnson & Allanson; Heiman Tischler, Barrouch Marks and Loeb Schlessinger—B. Marks & Co.; Matthew Lanfranco; Douglass, Foster & Wadhams; Juan T. Lanfranco, Louis Phillips, H. Hellman, Casper Behrend. In 1854, Adolph Portugal, O. W. Childs, Samuel Prager, Jacob Letter, M. Pollock and L. C. Goodwin—Pollock & Goodwin. 1855, Wolf Kalisher, Charles Prager, Potter & Co., Wm. Corbett, Geo. F. Lamson, P. C. Williams, J. G. Nichols, Dean & Carson, I. M. Hellman, B. Cohen and Morritz Schlessinger—Cohen & Schlessinger; L. Glaser & Co., Louis Cohen. 1856, Calisher & Cohen, Henry Wartenberg—W. Kalisher & Co., in 1857; Mendel Meyer, H. G. Yarrow. 1857, Samuel Hellman.

1859, Isaias W. Hellman, eminent since as banker, L. Leon, Corbett & Barker, Wm. Nordholt, David Solomon, H. Fleishman and Julius Sichel—Fleishman & Sichel. 1860, Edward Newman and Isaac Schlessinger, Jean B. Trudell—in company with Lazards; Domingo Rivara. 1861, M. W. Childs, December 20th.—The mercantile link continues to the present day as follows: J. H. Still & Co., booksellers and stationery, 1863; H. D. Barrows and J. D. Hicks —J. D. Hicks & Co., 1864; Eugene Meyer and S. Lazard—S. Lazard & Co., 1864; Polaski & Goodwin, 1865; Thomas Leahy, Samuel B. Caswell and John F. Ellis—Caswell & Ellis, 1866; Eugene Meyer and Constant Meyer—Eugene Meyer & Co. Potter & Co, consisted of Nehemiah A. Potter and Louis Jazinsky. The latter gentleman soon afterward went into business at San Francisco. Mr. Potter was born in 1809, at Cumberland, Rhode Island; he died at this city May 6th, 1868, leaving one son—Oscar Potter. George Alexander, in 1872, removed to Columbia, California. Francis Mellus was born at Salem, Massachusetts, February 3d, 1824; came to this coast, landing first at Santa Barbara, January 5th, 1839; died at Los Angeles City, September 11th, 1864. He married Miss Adelaida Johnson; she survives him, with seven children. Mrs. Mellus is a daughter of Don Santiago Johnson, an Englishman who had lived in Sonora, and come to this Coast in the year 1833. He married Dona Maria del Carmen Ginrado, sister of the wives of Don Manuel Requena and Alexander Bell. He died, at the age of 49 years, late in the Summer of 1846. Brought early in contact with men like A. B. Thompson, of Santa Barbara, David Spence, of Monterey, Abel Stearns, Alfred Robinson, W. D. M. Howard, and himself having received the ordinary Boston High School education of that day—which must have been good, for at 15 years he understood French and navigation, and was a neat draftsman—Mr. Mellus soon amassed the maxims of experience which fitted him to succeed in the California trade. His spirit and independence are worthy to be made a model by youth just entering among the currents and shoals of commercial life. "March 4th, 1839,—The Bolivar arrived from the islands," we quote from his diary: "March 9th.—I went aboard as clerk for Mr. Thompson, at $300 for the first year and $500 for the next, which I think is a most excellent salary for me. I hope from this time forward to be a burden to nobody, but look out for myself."

Bachmau & Co. invested deeply in the Salt Lake trade. Merchants were the soul of every enterprise formed to develop the resources and expand the commerce of this country. Fortunes were rapidly accumulated. Some sped away to fatherland to spend the rest of their days. Solomon Lazard having once more beheld "la belle France," returned, March, 1861, to our sunshine and flowers. Mendel Meyer studied the Vienna Exposition and wandered the world over in gratification of a rare musical taste, "but to feel better at home," as he often says. John Temple made the European tour in 1858. He was born at Reading, Mass., August 14, 1796; came to California in 1828, by way of the Sandwich Islands; died at San Francisco May 30, 1866. Dona Rafaela Cota, his widow, is at Paris. Juan T. Lanfranco, of Italy, died May 20, 1875; his brother Mateo, October 4, 1873. Prudent Beaudry arrived at San Francisco, April 26, 1850, and settled finally at Los Angeles, April 26, 1852. Beaudry's Block, on Aliso street, finished in November, 1857, was at the time a surprise. What may we have said to "Beaudry Terrace" and its oranges and other magical fruits of his energy? Edward Neuman, another merchant, in the bloom of youth, was murdered in 1863, on the Cucamonga plain.

In the explosion of the little steamer Ada Hancock, April 29th, 1863, near Wilmington, among many lost were, of our merchants, Wm. T. B. Sanford, Dr. Henry R. Miles, Loeb Schlessinger; with Capt. Thomas Seeley, of steamer Senator, Capt. J. S. Bryant, Fred Kerlin, Thomas Workman, the young Albert S. Johnston, son of Gen. Albert Sidney Johnston. Miss Medora Hereford, sister-in-law of Mr. B. D. Wilson, soon after died of injuries in this deplorable calamity.

From a list of foreigners dated May 23d, 1836, in the Los Angeles archives, we make an extract of the nativity, etc., of prominent persons who have acted—one of whom remains—upon the theatre which this sketch contemplates:

Name.	Nativity.	Date of Arrival.	Age.
J. J. Warner	United States	1831	28
N. Pryor	United States	1828	30
R. Laughlin	United States	1828	34
S. Prentice	United States	1829	37
L. Carpenter	United States	1833	22
L. Bouchet	France	1829	49
L. V. Prudhomme	France	1835	27
J. B. Leandry	Italy	1827	31
Santiago McKinly	Scotland	1824	33
D. Ferguson	Ireland	1824	30

Several of them were connected with large landed interests derived from the former Government. Poor Ferguson, old settler as he was, failed in 1836 to get even a town lot on his humble petition to the Ayuntamiento. Lemuel Carpenter bought Santa Gertrudes rancho from the Nieto heirs. He died November, 1859; Bouchet, October 23d, 1847; Pryor, May, 1850; Laughlin, December 6th, 1846; Prudhomme, May 8th, 1871. This is Nathaniel M. Pryor, frequently mentioned with favor in the local annals. The diary of Mr. Mellus has an entry touching his first wife, and is illustrative of the funeral custom of those days: "On Friday, September 4, 1840, at about four hours A. M., M. Pryor, an American, was deprived of his wife, only about 17 years of age, after a long sickness. On Saturday morning she was buried in the Church, on the left hand side, facing the altar." In 1845 the mother of Don Pio Pico was buried in the same manner. In 1847 the Priest proposed to pay this honor to Alfredo Flores, infant son of Gen. Jose Maria Flores, but the Ayuntamiento opposed it, and he was buried in the "Campo Santo," says the parish record. Pablo Pryor, of San Juan, is son of Nathaniel M. Pryor. The families of Richard Laughlin, and Leon Victor, Prudhomme reside in this city. Of all the foreigners resident here in the year 1845, there are living as follows: French—Pierre Domec, Antoine Laborie, Jose Mascarel, John Taite; Canadians—Elijah T. Moulton, Matias Bourke; Irish—D. W. Alexander, Dr. Richard S. Den; English—Henry Dalton, Michael White; Americans—B. D. Wilson, F. P. F. Temple, George Walters.

The arrival of the emigrants in El Monte gave the first decided impulse to agriculture in this county, encouraged business in the city of Los Angeles. and ever since has aided it materially. This great farming tract lies along the San Gabriel river, twelve miles east of the city. The soil in general does not need irrigation. There is much of interest in its history. Suffice to say, society is as well organized as in any part of the United States. The settlers of 1851, July, were Ira W. Thompson, Samuel M. Heath, Dr. Obed Macy and son, Oscar Macy, now residing in this city, F. W. Gibson, Nicholas Smith, J. Coburn, J. Sheldon,—Chisholm—and Mrs. John Roland, who now resides at Puente. Fifty odd families came in the year 1852, or early in 1853. We can mention but a few belonging to these two years: J. A. Johnson, William B. Lee, Samuel King and three sons (one of them Andrew J. King, Esq., of this city), Dr. T. A. Mayes, S. Bennett, A. Bacon, W. J. Willis, Edmond Tyler and two sons, John Thurman and seven sons, David Lewis, Wm. Rubottom, Ezekiel Rubottom, Samuel Thompson, Charles Cunningham, John Guess; Cudderback, Boss, the Hildreths. Jonathan Tibbetts came November 27, 1853; in 1852, Thomas A. Garey, since become the great horticulturist of this county. Adjoining El Monte, on the east, lies La Puente rancho, of 48,790 acres, granted July 22d, 1845, to John Roland and William Workman. Only a few miles further eastward is the fertile valley of San Jose, Los Nogales ranchito, about 500 acres, granted March 13, 1840, to Jose de la Cruz Linares; and next, San Jose de Palomares, of 22,720 acres, granted in the year 1837 to Ricardo Vejar, Ignacio Palomares and Luis Arenas. The grand railway trunk of the Southern Pacific runs through it to-day. It formed a connected settlement for several miles from near Roland's, chiefly of New Mexicans. This was a colony which John Roland gathered at Taos, Albuquerque and other pueblos of of New Mexico, in 1841. Under the leadership of Don Santiago Martinez they accompanied Mr. Roland in that year to California. A portion of them under Don Lorenzo Trujillo planted themselves at Agua Mansa, on the Santa Ana river, six miles south of San Bernardino, the rest in this valley. Time has made many changes since 1850, but has well tested the productiveness of its soil, upon which towns begin to flourish—Spadra, Pomona. *Cha-huiste,* or mildew, never affected the wheat of San Jose. Long after 1850, were to be seen the adobe ruins of the great granaries which the Padres built in front of William Workman's dwelling, to store the grain harvested on the plain of La Puente. The original settlement exists, missing many whose kindness memory cherishes—Ybarras, Alvarados, Martinez, * * * *

The foundation of the German colony at Anaheim in 1857, on what seemed a sandy waste, is an event, the magnitude of which we have not yet seen. Its founders designed the largest vineyard in the world. The first vines were set out in January and February, 1858, as indeed was perfected the whole plan, under the direction of George Hansen, Superintendent. It lies twenty-four miles south-east of this city. The first settlers were about fifty in number. The present population within and immediately surrounding it exceeds two thousand. It is the second town in the county. The colony was organized as above first mentioned as the "Los Angeles Vineyard Company," under a Board of Trustees in San Francisco; President, Otmar Caler; Vice-President, G. Ch. Kohler; Treasurer, Cayrus Beythien; Secretary, John Fischer. A ditch five miles in length, from Santa Ana, supplies water for all uses. While Anaheim was unconceived, Santa Ana, at Teodosio Yorba's gave the earliest grapes in the county; and up the river to Don Bernardo Yorba's, presented a settlement of Californians, contented and happy. Their loss was great when the head and front of everything useful or elegant among them had gone—Don Bernardo. He died November 20, 1858, a very large number of children and grand-children surviving him. His estate in part consisted of 7,000 head of cattle, of all classes, valued at $84,000, and his real property at $30,625, May 1, 1859. Don Teodosio Yorba, his brother, died February 5, 1863 The first through train of the Southern Pacific railroad, from Los Angeles to Anaheim, ran January 14, 1875 . Anaheim originally was part of the rancho San Juan Cajonde Santa Ana, granted May 13, 1837, to Don Juan Pacifico Ontiveras by Gov. Juan B. Alvarado.

The extensive territory comprised within San Bernardino formed part of Los Angeles county until the passage of the Act of the Legislature, approved April 26, 1853, which created that new county. Its organization was perfected under that Act by an election held according to notice of Messrs. Isaac Williams, David Seeley, H. G. Sherwood, and John Brown. A colony of Mormons was established in the year 1851 upon the site of the present city of San Bernardino, which was then a part of a tract of land granted June 21, 1842, by Gov. Juan B. Alvarado to Jose del Carmen Lugo, Jose Maria Lugo, Vicente Lugo, and Diego Sepulveda, containing eight leagues, or 35,510 acres. In November, 1851, Amasa Lyman and Charles Rich, Mormon Apostles, having completed their first payment of $13,000, entered into possession, and it was deeded to them February 15, 1852. That county includes former ranchos of Los Angeles county, as Chino, Cucamongo, Jurupa and others. The child has grown up to a vigorous manhood. The people have always been remarkable for industry, enterprise, and good financial management in public affairs. The separation was not injurious to the city of Los Angeles. Until within five or six years past, a brisk and valuable trade was carried on between the two places, in lumber, general agricultural produce, hides and wool—three-fourths on cash; and still there is some trade. San Bernardino county possesses vast resources, mineral and agricultural, that remain to be developed. There is no real antagonism of interests between these two counties, and the kindly sympathy of the past deserves to be fostered and preserved in future.

The policy of sub-division of the Mexican grants, which has so much aided agricultural progress in Los Angeles county, commenced in earnest in the year 1865, although earlier efforts were made in that direction. May 21, 1851, Henry Dalton, of Azusa, published a project for dividing two leagues, near 9,000 acres, into small farm lots, to suit purchasers, on the most favorable terms, with "a beautiful site for a town," which he intended laying out as soon as the wants of trade and settlers might require; and also to have a merchant flouring mill near by. Long since the promising settlement of Duarte has grown up in his neighborhood. October 22, 1852, John O. Wheeler offered in small farms of fifty acres, his rancho San Francisquito, near San Gabriel Mission. These proposals may have been premature, although there are some reasons to think that settlers might have taken them up more profitably than by wasting time, in some instances, upon supposed public land, the title to which is even now undetermined. In 1855, Don Antonio Maria Lugo, owner of San Antonio rancho, nearly 30,000 acres, lying between Los Angeles city and San Gabriel river, and finally granted to him in 1838, partitioned the same—reserving a homestead for himself—among his sons, Jose Maria, Felipe, Jose del Carmen, Vicente, Jose Antonio, and daughters, Dona Vicenta Perez, Dona Maria Antonia Yorba, and Dona Merced Foster. In 1860, Dona Merced Foster and Don Vicente Lugo sold their respective portions to parties who immediately resorted to sub-division and sales in small lots. The first deed is from Isaac Heiman, dated June 21, 1865, to David Ward; followed by several other sales in 1865 and 1866 to Jameson and others. But before this, Gov John G. Downey had commenced the sub-division of Santa Gertrudes rancho, lying along San Gabriel river and containing near 22,000 acres. His first deed is of date April 22, 1865, to J. H. Burke. Others followed to Neighbors and Hutchinson, and many afterward. This last is the locality known as Los Nietos. It had a settlement of over two hundred persons in 1836, broken up subsequently. Here is Downey City, twelve miles south-east from Los Angeles—a newspaper, business houses, a happy circle of farmers, with good title, upon a soil as rich as can be found on the face of the earth. This, with all the river land, and into El Monte, is our "corn county," emphatically. It deserves to be mentioned that Mr. Dalton did complete his promised flouring mill at Azusa, Oct. 19, 1855, and from wheat raised on his own rancho made an excellent quality of flour.

From 1850 to 1860, and thereabouts, the cattle trade and shipment of grapes were the main reliance for money. The cattle sold to go out of the county, in the former year, were estimated at 15,000 head, at $15 per head. Subsequent years, until 1856, show a constant demand for stock, if not so great; in this year it was considered that $500,000 had been invested in cattle and sheep, to be taken away. In 1860, there were still 78,000 head of cattle, three-fifths of which belonged to native Californians, and, in part, distributed as follows:

Abel Stearns, 12,000; Juan Abila, 7,200; John Roland, 5,000; William Workman, 5,000; Williams' estate, 5,000; John Temple, 4,000; Ricardo Vejar, 3,500; Bernardo Yorba, 3,500; Ignacio del Valle, 3,500; Teodosio Yorba, 3,500; Leonardo Cota, 2,500; Vicente Lugo, 2,500; Pio and Andres Pico, 2,000; Agustin Machado, 2,000; Nasario Dominguez's estate, 2,000; Felipe Lugo, 1.000; Valdez family, 1,000; Enrique Abila, 1,000; Fernando Sepulveda, 1,000.

Making just allowance for defective assessments, the amount was probably considerably—one third—beyond this estimate. The drought of the years 1863 and 1864, was more or less destructive throughout California. In Los Angeles County, 1865 began with 90,450 head of cattle, 15,529 horses, 282,000 sheep. In earlier times, sheep made little figure in the annual calculations of gain. In 1875, the total of flocks was counted at 508,757. From 1860 onward, wool became a staple, added to wine and brandy, orange and other fruits, wheat and corn. According to the Report of the County Surveyor, January 15th, 1876, the product of the wool was 2,034,828 pounds. Horned cattle were reduced to 13,000; horses, 10,000.

All the oranges in 1850 were from the Mission orchard of San Gabriel, and the gardens of Louis Vignes and William Wolfskill. June 7th, 1851,

Mr. Vignes offered for sale his "desirable property, El Alizo "—so called from the superb sycamore tree, many centuries old, that shaded his cellars. He says: " There are two orange gardens that yield from five to six thousand oranges in the season." It is credibly stated that he was the first to plant the orange in this city, bringing young trees from San Gabriel, in the year 1834. He had 400 peach trees, together with apricots, pear, apple, fig and walnut, and adds: " The vineyard, with 40,000 vines, 32,000 now bearing grapes, and will yield 1,000 barrels of wine per annum, the quality of which is well known to be superior." Don Louis came to Los Angeles, by way of the Sandwich Islands, in 1831—he was a native of France. One orange cultivator added after another, January 1st, 1876, there were in this county 36,700 bearing orange trees, and 6,900 bearing lime and lemon trees. The shipment of this fruit rapidly grew into a regular business. In 1851 there were 104 vineyards, exclusive of that of San Gabriel—all but 20 within the limits of the city. The San Gabriel vineyard, neglected since 1834, was now in decay. In Spanish and Mexican times, it had been called " mother vineyard," from the fact that it supplied all the original cuttings; it is said to have once had 50,000 vines. In 1875, the grape vines of this county were 4,500,000.

In 1851 grapes, in crates or boxes, brought 20 cents per pound at San Francisco, 80 cents at Stockton. Through 1852 the price was the same. This shipment continued several years, in general with profit. Very little wine was then shipped; in 1851, not over a thousand gallons. Soon the northern counties began to forestall the market with grapes nearly as good as our own. Gradually the manufacture of wine was established. Wolfskill indeed had, at an early date, shipped a little wine, but his aim was to turn his grapes into brandy. Louis Wilhart, in 1849 and 1850, made white wine considered, in flavor and quality, next to that of Vignes, who could produce from his cellars a brand perhaps unexcelled through the world. He had some in 1857 then over 20 years old—perhaps the same the army relished so well in 1847, as before intimated. Among the first manufacturers for the general market was Vincent Hoover, with his father, Dr. Juan Leonce Hoover, first at the 'Clayton Vineyard," which, owing to its situation on the bench, produced a superior grape; then from the vineyard known as that of Don Jose Serrano. Some of the vines in this last named, are stated to be 95 years old. This was from 1850 to about 1855. The cultivation of the grape too, about this time, took a new impulse. At San Gabriel, Wm. M. Stockton, in 1855, had an extensive nursery of grape vines and choice fruit trees. Dr. Hoover was an emigrant of 1849, by the Salt Lake route. He died October 8th, 1862, after a life somewhat eventful. He was born February 11th, 1792, in Canton Argau, Switzerland; graduated as a physician at Lyons, France; was surgeon in the army of Napoleon, and was at the burning of Moscow. Mrs. Eve Hoover, his wife, died September 11th, 1853, at the age of forty-one, a lady held in high esteem, and at whose death by an accident, the whole community was deeply affected. Joseph Huber, senior, came to Los Angeles for health from Kentucky. In the year 1855, he entered successfully into wine-making at the 'Foster vineyard.' He died aged 54 years, July 7, 1866; leaving a widow and six children, who reside at Los Angeles. Louis Wilhart died November 6th, 1871. April 14, 1855, Jean Louis Sansevaine purchased the vineyard property, cellars, etc., of his uncle, Louis Vignes, for $42,000 (by the by the first large land sale within the city). Mr. Sansevaine had resided here since 1853. In 1855 he shipped his first wine to San Francisco. In 1856 he made the first shipment from this county to New York, thereby becoming the pioneer of this business. Mr. Matthew Keller says: "According to the books of the great forwarding house of P. Banning at San Pedro, the amount shipped to San Francisco in 1857, was 21,000 boxes of grapes, averaging 45 pounds each, and 250,000 gallons of wine." In 1856 Los Angeles yielded only 7,200 cases of wine; in 1860 it had increased to 66,000 cases. In 1861 shipments of wine were made to New York and Boston by Benj. D. Wilson and J. L. Sansevaine; they are the fathers of the wine interest, Sunny Slope, unexcelled for its vintage—and the orange, almond and walnut—was commenced by L. J. Rose in January, 1861. December, 1859, the wine producers were: Matthew Keller, Sansevaine Bros., Frohling & Co.,

B. D. Wilson, Stevens & Bell, Dr. Parrott, Dr. Thos. J. White, Laborie, Messer, Barnhardt, Delong, Santa Ana precinct, Henry Dalton, P. Serres, Joseph Huber Sr., Ricardo Vejar, Barrows, Ballerino, Dr. Hoover, Louis Wilhart, Trabuc, Clement, Jose Serrano. The total manufacture of wine was about 250,000 gallons; in 1875, 1,328,900 gallons, according to the official report of the County Assessor, January 1st, 1876.

Mechanical industry exhibits a progress slow and difficult for the first few years. May 24, 1851, carpenters mostly had gone to San Francisco, where they could get higher wages. Early in 1850 Capt. Alexander Bell commenced Bell's Row, which is a number of well known little stores on Los Angeles street, and an improvement which at the time made a sensation. This work was done by James R. Barton and William Nordholdt (a man of '49,) through that and the succeeding year. After the election of Barton to the Sheriffalty Nordholdt carried on the business of carpenter until 1859, when he established himself in his present store. Feb. 19, 1853, Anderson & Matthews advertised as carriage makers, carpenters and joiners. William Abbott came in 1853 from New Albany, Indiana. October 1855, he started the furniture business in a little frame house about ten feet back from the street, which has grown into the stately building next to the Pico House, and the upper story of which is the handsome Merced Theatre—so named in honor of his wife, Dona Merced Garcia. William H. Perry arrived February 1st, 1853; in May 1855, he formed a partnership with Ira Gilchrist, as W. H. Perry & Co.; June, 1855, the firm was Perry & Brady—James D. Brady. June, 1858, Wallace Woodworth bought Brady's interest, under the style of Perry & Woodworth. Their business was inside, cabinet, etc. September 6th, 1861, Perry & Woodworth, Main street, had matured their pioneer saw and planing mills, with the manufacture of bee-hives, upholstery, etc., and were prepared for contracting, building and furnishing. In 1863 Stephen H. Mott entered into this firm. Eli Tayor, now of Los Nietos, was a carpenter in 1854. Others are as follows prior to 1859: George Stone, R. E. Jackson, George Leonard, Matthew Teed, Thomas Grey (a farmer well off now of the Cienega,) C. Perry Switzer, Peter Hendell, A. P. Bennett, William Coburn, P. C. Williams, Harris Niles, John McLimond, Willis Stanton, George Edgerton, W. Weeks, Antonio Heomle, William Cover, Herman Muller, Herman Koop, Charles Plaissant. House and sign painters, prior to 1859 were Wm. Shanning, Moses Searles, Charles Winston, Tom Riley, Forbes, Spilling, Viereck, Turnboldt; plasterers prior to 1857, Joseph Nobbs, Thos. Stonehouse, Wm. McKinney; Newton Foote came in that year. Andrew Lehman, shoemaker, set up business November 4th, 1852; it was three years before he began to "make a living." The stores engrossed the boot and shoe trade. He was born in the Grand Duchy of Baden, came across the plains by St. Joseph, and last from Cincinnati. One German shoemaker preceded him, but had left several months before. Afterward, prior to 1858 or 1859, came Morris and Weber. There was little to do for shoemakers until since 1860. B. J. Virgin was architect, 1855. Veireck, painter of political transparencies in 1852, left next year for want of employment; it must have been for some other reason, he turned comedian at San Francisco. January 17th, 1857, C. M. Kechnie was a portrait painter. Henri Penelon afterward was a distinguished artist.

John Goller, blacksmith and pioneer wagon-maker, was of the emigrants by the Salt Lake route. Louis Wilhart outfitted him with tools and helped him to customers. Iron works,as to cost,the native Californians were strangers to. One of them, as Goller used to say, paid $500 for an awning for the front of his residence. The charge for shoeing a horse was $16. Stores then were scarce of iron. Goller hunted up old tires thrown away on the plains to make shoes. His first wagon remained on hand a good while. The native people gazed at it with curiosity, but distrust, and went back to their carretas. Few carriages were made during the first six or eight years. E. L. Scott & Co. were carriage makers and blacksmiths in 1855. Louis Roeder came to Los Angeles November 29, 1856, worked nine years for Goller, then bought out J. H. Burke,who is now a wealthy citizen of Los Nietos, and in 1863, with William Schwartz, blacksmith, as partner, set up for himself on Main street. Ben McLaughlin also was a wheelwright. Among the early blacksmiths were Hiram McLaughlin, Charles F. Daley (killed by Pancho Daniel's band, January, 1857), Van Dusen; George Boorham, before 1856; Henry King, 1856. John Wilson came August 20, 1858, and set up for himself in 1868; James Baldwin, sometime after 1858. Of gunsmiths, Au gust Stoermer came in that year. He was preceded, March 16, 1855, by Henry C. G. Schaeffer. In the memory of old citizens, from his former familiar little adobe shop, it is a step into a garden where bloom choicest flowers of the world. He is all devoted, at sixty-five, to floriculture. Sam. C. Foy, Feb. 19, 1854, started his saddlery—the first to make any kind of harness. John Foy joined his brother in the following Summer. These spirited pioneers led the way soon to flourishing firms in the same line,—the young brothers Workman, Bell & Green, Heinche, D. Garcia.

The first bricks were made by Capt. Jesse D. Hunter in 1852. He burnt his next kiln in 1853. From the first kiln was built the house at the corner of Third and Main streets in 1853; from the second, in the same year, the new brick jail. In 1854 was built the Guadalupe Ross house, now of Samuel Meyer; in 1855 the dwelling and store of J. G. Nichols, on Main street near the Court House. Joseph Mullaly and Samuel Ayres, coming here March 1, 1854, embarked in brick-making the next month. In August, David Porter arrived. The firm then was, Mullaly, Porter & Ayers. In 1855, Jacob Wexel went to work for this firm on the Eagle Mills of Stearns & Scott, and the new brick dwelling of John Roland at La Puente. Their "great year" was 1858, when they sold 2,000,000 of brick for the proposed improvements of 1859. Besides the brick flouring mill of Stearns & Scott, were finished houses at various points for Foster & Wadhams, J. Morris, John Goller, Lorenzo Lecke, Juan Ramirez. From 1855 to 1859 there is a hiatus which cannot be better filled up than with the "Garden of Paradise," at the Round House, begun in 1856 by George Lehman, and which was a wonder to all by its mystic Adam and Eve, with the profusion of flowers and ingenious disposition of parterre and tree. In 1859 John Temple built and September 30, delivered to the city the market house, with its town clock and bell so "fine-toned and sonorous," at a cost of $40,000. He also constructed the south end of Temple Block. October 22, Don Abel rejoiced in the finishing touch to his prided undertaking, the Arcadia Block, bearing the name of his wife, Dona Arcadia Bandini; like the good ship Arcadia, Capt. Noyes, of Mr. Stearns and Alfred Robinson, that brought the second invoice of goods directly from Boston to San Pedro (the first, we are reminded, having been by the barque Eureka, Capt. Noyes, in the Fall of 1852, to Alexander & Mellus). In the same month, Corbett and Baker removed into the north-east corner store of the block, and it was soon filled. Then, too, the dining hall, just finished, of the Bella Union, was reported "one of the finest in California." The Mascarel building, now Polaski & Goodwin's, followed in 1861. The prevailing spirit awhile embraced the plaza within its range. It proved to advantage to all who heeded it, although good William Wolfskill had forebodings, in December, 1860, on the return from the burial of Henry Mellus—"What a pity!" he said; "if Temple had not built so much he might now be a rich man!" Mr. W. and Mr. T. died each probably worth a half a million. And at last Mr. W. himself ran with the tide and spent $20,000 to build the Lazard store, Main street, in 1866. It was completed by his executors.

So had some advancement been made, and public pride was animated. Twenty years before, one who deserves to be regarded as a Progressiveist, Regidor Don Leonardo Cota, 1845, April 19, had prayed the Ayuntamiento to petition the Governor for an order upon all the inhabitants "to plaster and whitewash the fronts of their houses." Satisfied if he could succeed in this, he said, "to have co-operated somewhat toward the glory of my country. The time had arrived," he thought, "for Los Angeles to figure in the political world, and although still a small city, to show its magnificence, so that the traveler coming to visit us might be able to say, 'I have seen the city of Los Angeles; I have seen its order and government, and all announce that it is to be the Paradise of Mexico;' but not so with the melancholy aspect of most of its buildings, dark and gloomy, and more like burial mounts of the ancient nomads than habitations for a free people." *

San Pedro, so noted as a port under the former regime, since 1850 has been, until recently, the only outlet for our productions. Ox carts could not remain long after the management of trade fell into the hands of Douglass & Sanford, John Goller, J. J. Tomlinson, J. M. Griffith, A. W. Timms, A. F. Hinchman, Don Jose Rubio, David W. Alexander, Phineas Banning, all of whom have done so much to build up our commerce. General Banning went there a young man. In 1851 was formed the firm of Alexanders & Banning, Commission and Forwarding Merchants. Subsequently for four years he conducted this business alone; marked by sagacity, foresight, and energy. In 1858, Old San Pedro was abandoned. Wilmington then became the real port for Los Angeles commerce. When he commenced, 500 tons would have been a fair average for the trips both ways per month. Now, there has been as high as 15,000 tons afloat at one time, to say nothing of the enormous amount of produce which the same vessels carried away on their departure. Gen. Banning has had the opportunity to see the passengers ride from the port to Los Angeles City on Mexican ox carts, with no iron in their construction, and has seen them at length make the trip on as fine railway cars as there are in the United States; and has seen them increase from fifty persons per month to near three thousand. With our best recollections of all the past, we think we may justly say, that no one of our citizens has contributed more of labor with perseverance, or more of business ability than he has done, to the accomplishment of this result. Gen. B. resides at Wilmington, in the bosom of his family. November 16th, 1854, he married Miss Rebecca Sanford. There are eight children of this marriage. February 22d, 1871, he married Miss Mary E. Hollister. They have three children.

Of the actors in scenes through which we have partly traveled, some are lost to sight: Don Jose Sepulveda, Don Manuel Requena, Don Andres Pico, Don Ignacio Alvarado, Don Augustin Machado, Louis Vignes, Isaac Williams, Andrew A. Boyle, John Roland, William Workman; others, many, whose names are dear to affection, and whose good deeds are treasured in universal respect. A. A. Boyle died, February 9th, 1871, aged 54 years; John Roland, at the age of 82 years, August 13th, 1873; William Workman, born with the century, died May 17th of the present year. Companions of a hundred dangers and toils, Roland and Workman sleep together, at La Puente, in the church-yard of the little chapel, which both designed many years ago. Don Jose Sepulveda, born November 30th, 1804, died in Mexico, April 17th, 1875. Don Andres Pico, born November 30th, 1810, died February 14th, 1876. A brother, Don Pio, and three sisters survive him—Dona Ysidora, wife of John Foster, Dona Concepcion, widow of Don Domingo Carrillo, Dona Maria, widow of Don Jose Joaquin Ortega. Don Pio Pico is another centenarian—if we may so speak; he was born at San Gabriel May 5th, 1800. Don Manuel Requena, born on the Peninsular of Yucatan, died at this city, aged 74 years, June 27th, 1876. Don Andres Pico and Don Jose Sepulveda were born at the Old Presidio of San Diego. Isaac Williams, born in Wyoming Valley, Pennsylvania, September 19, 1799, died at Chino Rancho, September 13th, 1856; he came to California in the year 1832. Aged 91 years, Louis Vignes died January 17th, 1862; at near the same age, September 25th, 1858, Don Ignacio Abila, and more recently Don Julio Verdugo. John Goller died July 7th, 1874. Don Agustin Machado died May 17th, 1865, at 77 years of age. One of a company—the others, Felipe Talamantes, Tomas Talamantes, and his own brother, Ignacio Machado—who in 1839 received a grant of the Rancho of La Ballona. Don Ignacio survives those faithful friends of his earlier days—at the age of 82 years; he grasps the hand warmly as ever, rides on horseback as usual—patriarch to whom the community bears respect almost filial. Don Ignacio Palomares, born February 2d, 1811, died November 25, 1864, and at close to 70 years, May 6th, 1876,

---

* See Historical Collection, San Francisco, of Hubert H. Bancroft, Esq., which has full records of early history of Los Angeles and Southern California in general, and from which we have drawn liberally the facts of the present sketch for the period since 1817.

his friend, Don Ignacio Alvarado—guides and lights in life both of a trusting people through all the peaceful Valley of San Jose.

William Wolfskill was born March 20, 1798, near Richmond, Ky.; his grand-father, from Germany, and grand-mother, from Ireland; came to Los Angeles in 1830. Aged seventy-five years, he died at this city Oct. 3, 1866, leaving four children. He planted his original vineyard in 1838. He believed that, well cared for, the grape vine will last a hundred years. He had been often heard to say that his first orange orchard, the small one near the old adobe dwelling, was of the same age of his eldest daughter, Juana, who was born in 1841. His wife, Dona Magdalena Lugo, of Santa Barbara, died before him. His daughter Juana was married November 14, 1860, to H. D. Barrows, and died January 31, 1863. Her husband and one daughter reside at this city. Alexander Bell was born in Washington county, Penn., January 9, 1801. In 1823 he went to the city of Mexico, was a merchant until 1842, when he came, by the way of Guaimas, to San Pedro. In 1844 he married Dona Nieves Guirado, who survives him. He died July 24, 1871. They were without children; but they were *Padrinos* (god-father and god-mother) to more children than any other couple in California. "Thus they sustained the pleasant relation," says Mr. H. D. Barrows, "to a large number of fathers and mothers, so common in Spanish, although unknown in English, of *compadre* and *comadre*. And although some of their god-children have grown up to be men and women, while others are still infants, these old people always welcomed them at meeting, great or small, with as much interest and affection apparently as would have been done had they been their own children." It is one simple picture of "California life" as it is at Los Angeles; where this double family tie, (as it were) serves to elevate personal intercourse, and strengthens and beautifies all the social relations.

Twenty years of existence, while awakening curiosity, leave hints for instruction. Errors we have committed. The race of fortune has been checked suddenly,—by commercial shocks, by other causes beyond human power to avert. A dry season of 1856 and 1857, money depression in 1859, drought through 1863 and 1864, and varied drawbacks by sea and land, now bad modes of agriculture and want of skill in wine manufacture; again, disappointment in mining experiments at Kern river, San Gabriel and elsewhere, and ineffectual, although masterly efforts for the Salt Lake trade, with expensive, disheartening litigation for "the ranchos," all have retarded the onward march. In vain, lament these failures of realization where hope was so much excited, or renew the torments of evils which time has cured. Gone, too, with the past, are personal or political rivalries, that have lost their interest for the public. Questions of grave import as they may have been, give way to themes nearer to our present well-being. If there have been other critical years beset by solicitude and fear, of this great day are born only glorious inspirations, rejoicing all in one common country, under one Union—indivisible, perpetual!

CHAPTER III.

Los Angeles County From 1867 to July 4th, 1876.

HE third period, or age, in the history of Los Angeles may be said to have commenced with the tide of immigration which set in for Southern California about the year 1866.

The first era had been the long, slumb'rous years of the old Missions and ranchos, when life was a thing of dreamy days and peaceful nights; when no sound of hurry or of toilsome labor disturbed the quiet; when the drowsing pueblo and the sleeping hacienda only aroused to the bustle of an occasional fiesta or rodeo; when, instead of the black smoke of the steamer, leaving its long trail over the waters, only the white sails of the hide drogher, at intervals of many long months, broke the blue stretch of the sea. This era must ever remain to the mind of the dreamer, the poet, the halcyon age of California del Sur.

The second period embraces the time from the American occupation of California to about the year 1866. This era was also one of sharply defined characteristics. An influx of a new race, of new men, not great in numbers but of marked individuality, took place. The sun-tanned trappers, keen of eye and strong of limb, began to straggle in, coming from the mystery of the unexplored heart of the continent, as denizens of another world who by some mischance had dropped upon this planet. Men wise in the strange, unworldly wisdom that comes not of schools nor of trade, but of lone years lived by the rivers, among the canons, where the only voice of converse is the voice of the night wind among the sombre pines. Other men came too—sharp witted men who saw gold in the broad acres of the great ranchos, even as their contemporaries saw it in the sands of the rivers of Alta California.

Still, the great mass of population remained unchanged, and, while the new element organized business, reached out to the interior, to Arizona, to Salt Lake, for trade, yet outside of the pueblos the slumber of the old rancho life was hardly disturbed. The towns, however, stirred to the new spirit and began to cast off their lethargy. Sail vessels and then steamships began to frequent the ports. Steamer day usurped the place of "poco tiempo" in the reckonings of trade. Men of business sagacity began quietly to secure large tracts of land, and real estate in the towns, foreseeing the rapid enhancement of values which must soon take place. The immigration was not always made up of the more peaceable elements of society. Men of questionable character, men of no character, drifted in. Money was plentiful, and the gamblers found a congenial field. The revolver shared with the Courts in the settlement of disputes. It is even reported that during a session of one of the Courts, the majesty of the law failed to repress the instinctive reliance of the American sovereign upon his weapons. Pistols were drawn, and the Judge, after vainly commanding the peace, rushed half way up the stairs out of harm's way, and peeping cautiously over the railing at the angry disputants below, testily called out: "Now shoot, and be d—d to you!" It was a time, too, of practical joking; jokes oftentimes sadly trying to the nerves of innocent visitors from abroad. It is related that once upon a time, as several of the leading citizens were entertaining a party of visitors, newly arrived, in one of the saloons where the *ton* were wont to resort, doing the honors of the city to the strangers, possibly initiating them into the delightful mysteries of draw poker—anyhow, it was said that everything was lovely and serene, when a noise at the door attracted their attention, racing to get in first, horses on the gallop, and in the gaze met the grim eyes of a townsman gloomily glancing at them along the sights of a shot-gun that looked like a double-barreled columbiad, while a determined voice muttered, "I'll shoot, even if I don't kill more than half a dozen!" The visitors were called by urgent business to San Francisco the next day, and, it is said, forgot to return. Railroads were then a thing of the future. The writer vividly recollects standing in front of the U. S. Hotel, in 1868, one night of a steamer's arrival, and hearing the rival stages of Banning and Tomlinson come up Main street, racing to get in first, horses on the gallop, and in the darkness a man on each stage blowing a horn to warn people in the street to clear the track. At this time, the Fall of 1868, there was no three story building in the town, while the only two story business houses were the old Lafayette, the older portion of the Bella Union, with the stores of Barrows and Childs upon Los Angeles street, Stearn's Block, Bell's Block, a portion of the Lanfranco building, the older portion of the U. S. Hotel, Allen's corner, the Court House with the part of Temple Block facing it, and a two story adobe where Temple's Bank now stands. The portion of Downey Block facing toward the Temple Bank had a few one story adobe rooms, with a wide gateway in the middle opening into a corral. This gateway had connected with it somewhat of a tragic history, as, upon the cross-bar above, five desperadoes were hanged at one time by the Vigilance Committee. The Round House was then upon the outskirts of town. Captain Clark's house was fairly in the country, but little of the property around being even fenced in. The hills above town and across the river, now dotted with houses, were then bleak and bare. East Los Angeles had not yet even been dreamed of. Between Los Angeles and Wilmington, instead of the many farms that now dot the country, were only a few ancient ranche houses, and the midway stations for changing horses on the stage routes. Los Angeles, Wilmington, Anaheim, El Monte and San Gabriel, might be called the only settlements. Lands where Compton now stands were sold at from $3 to $5 per acre. The total assessed valuation of property in the county for the year 1866 was $2,366,886. For the year 1875, nine years later, it stands $14,890,765. Population of the county for 1866 is estimated at 10,000. For 1875 it is probably 30,000. Of this population, about 5,000 then lived in the city of Los Angeles; now it is estimated the city has about 13,000.

In the year 1867 Los Angeles was first lighted with gas. During this year, also, Doctor Griffin and Hon. B. D. Wilson, by means of a ditch, costing some $15,000, brought the water of the Arroyo Seco out upon the lands of the San Pasqual rancho.

In the year 1868 work was commenced by the "Canal and Reservoir Co." upon the canal and reservoir which now supply the woolen mill. This was the first turning of attention to the hill lands west of the city, which before were considered practically valueless. This year marked an era in the business of the Southern portion of the county, in that, for the first time, Anaheim Landing was made a regular stopping place by steamers. This was the year, too, in which the first successful artesian well was bored in the county. A fair flow of water was obtained upon the mesa lands about six miles back of Wilmington. The well was sunk upon the property of Messrs. Downey and Hellman. So great a curiosity was it considered that the stages turned aside from the road to give passengers a sight of it. One other event, and most important of all, renders this year memorable in the history of the industrial development of Los Angeles. This was the carrying of the vote to issue county bonds for $150,000, and city bonds for $75,000, to assist in the building of a railroad from the city of Los Angeles to San Pedro harbor. This was the first step in the development of the railroad system which is now so rapidly opening up the resources of Southern California. And yet this road, only 22 miles in length, was looked upon by many as a foolish undertaking which would never pay expenses. One old resident, a man of wealth, contemptuously declared that two trains a month would accommodate all the wants of trade for years to come. Six years later the number of cars arriving daily at the Los Angeles depot with freight from Wilmington averaged, for weeks at a time, from fifty to sixty. This year settlers began to come in rapidly upon the lands about Compton, the town receiving its name from one of the first and most prominent of the new comers. The lands thrown upon the market by Governor Downey at Los Nietos were also quickly settled by an industrious farming population. In July of this year the "Los Angeles City Water Company," represented by Dr John S. Griffin, Mr. P. Beaudry and Mr. S. Lazard, received a franchise for supplying the city with water for domestic purposes for a period of thirty years, and, by agreement, and purchase of existing works, became possessed of a sole right. Previous to 1863 the city was poorly supplied, carts hauling water from the zanjas and from the river, and distributing it to the houses. In that year Jean L. Sansevaine, under franchise from the city, laid down wooden pipes in a few of the streets, which, however, soon became rotten and worthless. Since the introduction of pure water into the city, dysentery, which had been exceedingly prevalent, has become a rare disease. The "Los Angeles City Water Co." now represents a capital of $930,000. It has in the ground 24 miles of mains, the largest being 22 inches in diameter; daily consumption of water, 750,000 gallons; daily capacity, 1,000,000 gallons; estimates that it can supply a city of 100,000 inhabitants; expects to construct during the ensuing year another reservoir, 60 feet higher than the present one, to supply the hill lands. During the autumn of this year there was an unusual prevalence of a severe form of typho-malarial fever, many cases terminating fatally. In this year, 1868, the first bank was organized in Los Angeles by Alvinza Hayward and John G. Downey, under the firm name of "Hayward & Co.," capital, $100,000. Later in the same year the banking house of "Hellman, Temple & Co." was organized; capital, $125,000. By the reorganization and consolidation of these two houses, in February, 1871, was established the "Farmers' and Merchants' Bank of Los Angeles," with a capital at present of $500,000.

The years 1869 and 1870 were years of no marked events. During the year 1869 an epidemic of small-pox lingered for many months about the city. The winters of 1869-70 and 1870-71 were remarkable for a very light rain-fall, the first having less than nine and the second less than eight inches, with much dry northerly and westerly wind and frequent sand-storms. Despite these draw-backs a steady development went on, though the drought prevented the inauguration or prosecution of enterprises involving any heavy expenditure of money. "The Anaheim Gazette" was established in September.

In the year 1871, after several careful preliminary surveys, the United States Government commenced the work of improving Wilmington harbor, which work has ever since been going steadily on. $425,000 have so far been appropriated for the breakwater and the clearing out of the bar. When work was commenced the bar had upon it only 18 inches of water at low tide, and was only crossed by lighters which waited for the flood. While this historical sketch is in press, a fleet of 15 vessels, some drawing more than 13 feet of water, is lying within the harbor, having crossed the bar without the slightest difficulty. When the work is completed the engineers expect to give at least 17 feet of water upon the bar at low tide, and probably more. To the indefatigable exertions of Gen. P. Banning of Wilmington is due, more than to the efforts of any other one man, the inauguration of this work. With its completion the railroad system of Los Angeles will be enabled to reach its true fullness of development. This same year, was commenced, by Messrs. Chapman and Glassell, the construction of a system of canals for the irrigation of lands of the "Santiago de Santa Ana" rancho, upon the east side of the Santa Ana river. The main canal, constructed principally in this and the following years, is now some 15 miles in length, and with its various ramifications furnishes water for about 15,000 acres in the flourishing settlements of Orange, Tustin City and Santa Ana. In January of this year the "Los Angeles Medical Asssociation" was organized, the first medical society ever established in the county. It still retains its organization, and is in a flourishing condition. In February was issued the first number of the "Los Angeles Daily Evening Express."

In the year 1872 improvements were commenced in the hills West of Los Angeles city. These hills, although offering delightful sites for residences, from lack of water and difficulty of access, had not shared in the prosperity of the city, but had remained comparatively valueless and neglected. To the energy and perseverance, more especially of two men, Mr. P. Beaudry and Mr. J. W. Potts, is due the change that has taken place. Mr. Potts has, since 1872, expended in grading, principally upon the lines of Temple and Second streets, upwards of $30,000. Mr. Beaudry has in like manner expended upwards of $50,000. The work with which Mr. Beaudry's name has been more especially linked is the furnishing of an abundant supply of water to these hill lands. Mr. Beaudry has had excavated a large basin amid the springs lying along upper Alameda street, from which, with a sixty horse power engine running a Hooker pump of the capacity of 40,000 gallons per hour, water is forced to an elevation of 240 feet, where it is received by two reservoirs with a storage capacity of 3,500,000 gallons, and thence distributed through eleven miles of iron pipes over the tops of the highest hills. These works have cost $95,000. This year was founded the "Temple and Workman Bank." By firemen it will be remembered as the year in which the first fire-engine was brought to Los Angeles—a 2d class steamer, made by the Amoskeag Co. "La Cronica" issued its first number August 4th.

Eighteen hundred and seventy-three is memorable as the year in which Los Angeles county, by formal vote of the people, determined to go on in the work of perfecting a system of railroads; this, too, at a time when elsewhere over the country the war upon railroads was bitter and wide-spread. The county voted to the Southern Pacific R. R. Co. its bonds in the San Pedro railroad, and an additional amount sufficient to make up about 500,-000, upon the conditions that the main trunk line of S. P. R. R., on its way to connect with any southern trans-continental line, should pass through the Los Angeles valley; that the Company should within eighteen months have constructed fifty miles of railroad within the county, and within two years thereafter should also connect Los Angeles and Anaheim by rail, and that a connecting line through to San Francisco should be finished within three years. The city of Los Angeles also voted her interest in the San Pedro road, amounting to $75,000, upon condition that the main trunk line should pass through the city, and within certain specified limits. The Southern Pacific R. R. Co. has more than kept faith with the people of Los Angeles. Not only has it completed the 70 miles contemplated in the contract, but it has gone on building until Los Angeles is now the center of a system of more than 200 miles of road, and the work of extending the lines goes actively on. The construction of these roads has added millions to the wealth of the county, and is rendering possible other changes of still greater moment in the near future. This year iron pipes were first extensively used, instead of open ditches, in conducting water for irrigating purposes. The "Orange Grove Association," often called the "Indiana Colony," having purchased a portion of the San Pasqual rancho, piped the water out to their reservoir and thence by distributing pipes over the lands. Previous to this time, however, Mr. L. H. Titus, of San Gabriel, had demonstrated upon a smaller scale at his orchards the economy of such a system. Dr. Griffin and Governor Downey, at a heavy personal expense, laid water pipes over what is now East Los Angeles, and put the lands upon the market. During this summer the high school building upon the hill was erected, and under the efficient supervision of Dr. Lucky, as Superintendent, a thorough system of grading was adopted in the schools, which speedily gained an enviable reputation among the educational institutions of the State. No small share of credit in the erection of the high school building, and in the previous development of the schools from a chaotic condition, is due to Dr. T. H. Rose, a man of singular merit as an educator, who resigned from his connection with the schools in the summer of this year. In January the "Los Angeles Public Library" opened its doors; an institution supported by private membership, but to the rooms of which all are made welcome. Among the influences at work refining, elevating, ennobling public sentiment in community, the power of this library has not been least, though its work has ever been quiet and unobtrusive. From its first opening to the present it has remained in charge of Mr. J.C.Littlefield as Librarian. In April was organized the oldest fire company now existing in Los Angeles, the "Thirty-Eights, Fire Co. No. 1;" so called from the number of chartered members. In the summer was laid the corner stone of the Synagogue B'nai-Brith, by the Hebrew Society, under the pastorate of Rabbi A. W. Edelman. In the autumn was built, by Barnard Bros., the first woolen mill. In August the "Los Angeles Chamber of Commerce" was incorporated; an organization which has done, and is yet doing, a valuable work in the industrial and commercial development of Los Angeles County. October 2d was issued the first number of the "Daily Herald." In the previous January publication was commenced of the "Weekly Mirror."

Among events of the year 1874 may be mentioned the following: Don Benito D. Wilson and Mr. J. De Barth Shorb commenced piping water out to several large reservoirs, which they had constructed upon the plains near the Mission San Gabriel, thus supplying water for the "Alhambra" tract, which, from its choice location, is rapidly becoming the home of wealthy and refined families. Hon. Chas. Maclay purchased the San Fernando rancho, and founded the town of the same name. The first fruit-drying factory was built in Los Angeles by Mr. G. B. Davis. Prospecting and boring for petroleum was commenced in the mountains about San Fernando. The First Presbyterian Church was organized in Los Angeles city under the pastorate of Dr. A. F. White. "Trinity" M. E. Church South was erected under the pastorate of Rev. A. M. Campbell. In the Summer of this year was built, mainly through the personal efforts of Judge R. M. Widney, President of the Company, the first street railroad in Los Angeles, the "Spring and Sixth St.," some two and one-half miles in length. Since then have been built the Main street road, the East Los Angeles road, the San Pedro street road, work has been commenced upon the Aliso street road, and a road has been chartered upon Spring street. The "Los Angeles Savings Bank" was opened this year, capital $300,000; and the "Confidence Fire Co. No. 2" organized with another steamer, of the Amoskeag 2d class pattern. July 25th the first number of the "Sued Californische Post" appeared. It is a noteworthy fact in the history of the year that Los Angeles was, so far as known, the only city in the State, except one, in which a full compliance with the requirements of the "Sunday Law," passed by the preceding Legislature, was enforced. Business houses were closed, and from that time the Sabbath has been kept by the community as a day of rest.

In the Spring of 1875 the "Forest Grove Association" planted the first extensive tract of the Eucalyptus or blue gum, for timber. With this year was commenced the construction of another railroad. Senator John P. Jones, selecting Santa Monica roadstead as the ocean terminus, and running a substantial wharf out half a mile to deep water, built at a total outlay of some $375,000, a railroad to Los Angeles city. This section is intended as only the first portion of a road to be extended on through the Cajon Pass to Independence, and ultimately to be connected with the Union Pacific. With the building of this road has grown up a prosperous sea-side town at Santa Monica, much frequented as a watering place. During the Summer the Pomona and Artesia Companies placed upon the market several large tracts of land, subdivided into small farms. In the Southern part of the county the canals about Anaheim, and upon the west side of the Santa Ana, were rapidly extended for the irrigation of a number of thousands of acres of land before uncultivated. Anaheim, Westminster, Richland, Los Nietos, El Monte, Compton, Florence, and numerous other settlements over the county, were all the while rapidly increasing in wealth and population. Newport, south of the Santa Ana river, began to build up a direct trade with San Francisco, a steam schooner, owned by McFadden Bros., making regular trips. In March was first published the "Los Nietos Valley Courier;" in April, "El

Monte Observer;" in September, the "Santa Monica Outlook." The financial
crash which swept over the State during this year did not spare Los Angeles.
The three banks closed their doors for a short time.   Two re-opened with
strength unimpaired; the third, after struggling for a while, finally succumbed and made an assignment.   Under the pastorate of Rev. J. M. Campbell, the new edifice of the "Fort street M. E. Church" was erected, but dedi-
cated in the autumn, in the ensuing Conference year, during the pastorate of
the Rev. G. S. Hickey.   The Cathedral of "Sancta Vibiana" was reared by
the Rt. Rev. Thadeus Amat, but not opened to public service until the Spring
of 1876.   The steady development of an enlightened public sentiment is
shown by the general approbation expressed at the strong stand taken by
His Honor, P. Beaudry, Mayor of the city of Los Angeles, in his message
upon the questions of a liberal support of the public school system, the importance of a well sustained department of public health, and the duty of the
city in checking the vice of intemperance by restrictions upon the sale of
intoxicating liquors.

The year 1876, the Centennial of American Independence, and the 105th
since the first Mission was founded in the county, at San Gabriel, has so far
been marked by no striking events.   The "Commercial Bank of Los Angeles" opened its doors in January.   The 10th of the same month, publication
of the "Evening Republican" was commenced.   A plenteous and well distributed rainfall has insured an abundant harvest; the area of land under
cultivation is much larger than ever before; no blight has come upon the
broad fields; the promise has held good, "Seed time and harvest" have not
failed; while the hand of God has been in our midst, and there have been
tears, and aching hearts, even as alway, yet, the shadow of no pestilence has
rested upon our homes. And all the while the sun has not forgotten to shine,
nor the morning to come again; and the land has had peace; and rest and
plenty have reigned within our borders.   It is meet and proper, therefore, as
recommended by our Chief Magistrate, that each one should, after the manner of his own faith, return thanks to the one God of us all; meet and proper
that old hatreds, old enmities, should be buried with the dead century, to be
remembered no more through all the years, and that, over the graves of our
dead, hands should clasp with only one word, Peace!

APPENDIX.

THE FIRST CENTENNIAL CELEBRATION

OF THE

DECLARATION OF INDEPENDENCE

BY THE

UNITED STATES OF AMERICA,

AT THE

CITY OF LOS ANGELES, STATE OF CALIFORNIA,

JULY FOURTH, 1876.

AT A MEETING OF CITIZENS, on Saturday evening, April 29th, 1876, Mr. James J. Ayers, having been chosen President, stated that the object of the meeting was to consider the matter of the due celebration of the approaching Centennial Anniversary of the Independence of the United States. Messrs. Chas. E. Miles, John R. Brierly, and Elijah H. Workman were appointed a committee to prepare and report a plan for the proper celebration of the coming event. The meeting then adjourned for one week.

The proceedings of the adjourned meeting, which was held May 6th, and published in the papers of the next morning, were as follows:

The largest meeting of the kind ever held in this city took place last night at the County Court room. At a quarter past eight it was called to order by President J. J. Ayers, who stated that the meeting was an adjourned one, and it was ready to receive the report of the committee appointed on Thursday night last.

Mr. Brierly, from the Committee of Three, read a preliminary report, which was adopted.

The following is the report:

We recommend for the celebration a grand procession of all the citizens of Los Angeles County.

In addition to the usual literary exercises, we favor a historical sketch of Los Angeles County.

We consider the following committees should be appointed, and recommend the citizens we name for the various committees:

Executive Committee—C. C. Lips, Samuel Meyer, E. H. Workman, Wm. Ferguson, I. A. Dunsmoor, L. Polaski, Chas. Prager, A. J. Johnston, E. E. Hewitt, J. U. Crawford, Los Angeles; Gen. George Stoneman, San Gabriel; Gen. Phineas Banning, Newport; George Hinds, Esq., Wilmington; S. C. Hough, Esq., Santa Monica; James McFadden, Esq., Santa Ana; Judge Holloway, Los Nietos; Edward Evey, Esq., Anaheim.

Literary Committee—Hon. Y. Sepulveda, A. James, E. M. Ross, J. Graves, H. T. Hazard, J. P. Widney, M. J. Newmark, Los Angeles; J. M. Guinn, Anaheim; T. A. Saxon, La Ballona.

Finance Committee—John Milner, C. W. Gould, M. Kremer, Charles R. Johnson, W. J. Brodrick, Horace Burdick, M. Teed.

Fireworks and Decorations Committee—C. E. Miles, Constant Meyer, T. E. Rowan, Peter Thompson, C. E. Huber, F. B. Fanning, C. E. Judd, Mr. Koster.

Collection Committee—Jos. Coblentz, John Kuhrts, Joseph Huber, John J. Carrillo, G. E. Gard, Aaron Smith, A. H. Denker, J. S. Tam, Louis Wolfskill, Geo. Furman.

Commissary Committee—Gabriel Allen, A. C. Chauvin, J. H. Seymour, Los Angeles; O. H. Burke, Los Nietos; J. Cohen, Anaheim; Geo. Carson, Compton; B. S. Eaton, San Gabriel; W. W. Rubotom, Spadra.

Respectfully submitted,

CHARLES E. MILES,
JOHN R. BRIERLY,
E. H. WORKMAN.

Mr. J. J. Ayers was then elected Permanent President, and Mr. B. C. Truman was selected as Permanent Secretary.

Mr. Miles, from the Committee of Three, asked for further time to elaborate and perfect their report, which was granted, provided that it was completed by the next meeting.

Mr. Hubbel thought it would be a good thing to send circulars to the prominent men in the county, and he made a motion to that effect.

Mr. Hubbell's resolution was adopted.

A motion then prevailed that posters should be put up throughout the county requesting the people to elect delegates on Saturday, the 13th instant, who should meet the Los Angeles people at the Court House on the Saturday following, the 20th instant, at 11 o'clock A. M.

The Executive Committee was directed to have the posters and circular letters printed and sent according to the resolution.

The meeting then adjourned.

The Literary Committee met in the evening of May 12th, at the chambers of Judge Sepulveda, and made the following appointments: General Phineas Banning, President of the Day; Col. James G. Eastman, Orator of the Day; J. J. Ayers, Poet; Messrs. J. J. Warner, Judge Benj. Hayes, and J. P. Widney were appointed a committee to prepare a historical sketch of the County of Los Angeles, to be furnished the respective papers (and not to be read) on the morning of the Fourth of July; Thomas A. Saxon, Reader of the Declaration of Independence, and the Revs. Mr. Edelman and Packard Chaplains.

Meeting on May 20th.

The Centennials met May 20th at the County Court House, Mr. J. J. Ayers, President, in the chair, B. C. Truman Secretary, and a large number of gentlemen present.

The object of the meeting was to receive the reports of the Committees for the purpose of ratification or rejection, and to meet the delegates from the outside districts.

On motion, Mr. Timms, of Old San Pedro, was added to the Executive Committee; also Messrs. Quinn and Tipton, of El Monte.

The following report of the Executive Committee was unanimously adopted :

Los Angeles, May 13th, 1876.

Gentlemen.—We submit the following report of our proceedings this day :

For Grand Marshal—Major H. M. Mitchell.
Committee on Invitation—E. E. Hewitt, A. J. Johnson and C. C. Lips.
Committee on Music—C. C. Lips, E. Workman and R. Dillon.

The Literary Committee presented the following report to the Executive Committee, which that Committee read to the meeting:

Los Angeles, May 13th, 1876.

To the Executive Committee for the coming Centennial Celebration:

Gentlemen.—At 8 o'clock p. m., Friday, May 12th, 1876, the Committee on Literary Exercises met pursuant to the call of the Chairman.

Present—Hon. Y. Sepulveda, Alfred James, E. M. Ross, J. A. Graves, H. T. Hazard, J. P. Widney, M. J. Newmark and Thos. A. Saxon.

T. A. Saxon was elected as Secretary, and the following gentlemen were elected as literary officers of the day : ·

President—Gen. P. Banning.
Orator—Hon. Jas. G. Eastman.
Poet—J. J. Ayers.
Historians—Col J. J. Warner, Judge Benj. Hayes, and Dr. J. P. Widney.

The duties of the historians are to furnish a condensed history of Los Angeles city and county for the press on the day of celebration.

Chaplains—Opening prayer, Rev. T. T. Packard; benediction, Rev. A. W. Edelman.   Thos. A. Saxon, Secretary.

By order of the Literary Committee.

Centennial Order.

Grand Marshal's Office, Los Angeles, Cal., June 29th 1876.

The procession with which the Fourth of July, 1876, will be celebrated in this city will be composed of four divisions, and will be formed at 9:30 a. m. on that day in the following order:

The First Division will form with its right on Fort street, at the intersection of Fifth.

The Second Division on Fort street at the intersection of Fourth.

The Third Division on Fort street at the intersection of Third.

The Fourth Division on Fort street at the intersection of Second.

The intersecting streets will be used for assembly, and Marshals of Divisions, with their aids, will be on duty at the points above indicated on the morning of the Fourth at 9 o'clock, and until 9:30, for the purpose of receiving the participants in the procession assigned in their respective Divisions. The procession will start promptly at 10 o'clock a. m., and will take the following route through the city:

From Fort street down Fifth to Spring; up Spring to Main; Main to Commercial; down Commercial to Los Angeles; on Los Angeles to Aliso; down Aliso to the Aliso Mills, where the procession will countermarch and be reviewed by the Grand Marshal; thence up Aliso street to Los Angeles; across Los Angeles and through Arcadia to Main; up Main to and around the Plaza, and returning down Main street to the Round House Gardens, at which place the literary exercises of the day's celebration will be held. At the conclusion of the exercises the procession will not be reformed, each participant being left at liberty to return to hall or home by any route preferred. The following named Marshals of Divisions have been appointed, each to appoint six aids to serve on his staff:

Marshal of the First Division—John F. Godfrey.
Marshal of the Second Division—Otto Von Ploennies.
Marshal of the Third Division—Eugene Meyer.
Marshal of the Fourth Division—Francisco Guirado.

The insignia to be worn by Marshals and aids are: Grand Marshal, red sash, star on left breast, black feather in hat, and baton. Aids, red, white and blue sash and black feather.

Marshals of Division: Blue sash, tri-color rosette on left breast, black feather and baton. Aids, red, white and blue sash and black feather.

Positions in the procession will be assigned on Saturday the 30th inst.

H. M. MITCHELL,
Grand Marshal.

The Celebration of the Centennial.

From the newspapers of the day following the celebration, the report of the proceedings has been compiled. The patriotism of the people of Los Angeles found a most fitting expression in the ceremonies. Preparations for the celebration of the Centennial anniversary of the Declaration of American Independence had been going on for some time, but it was not until the long line of the procession was formed that our citizens knew how complete they had been, or how perfectly success had characterized the efforts of the various committees. The public spirit of the citizens was made manifest by the beauty of the

PRIVATE DECORATIONS

Of stores, hotels and residences. To enumerate all the buildings which attracted attention by the profuse and tasty display of bunting, would be to give a catalogue of two-thirds of the houses in town. From one end of Main street to the other the display was very noticeable.

The Pico House led the van in the extent and elegance of adornment. In front of the building the proprietors had erected a column about feet high, surmounted by a flag-staff bearing a liberty cap. On the four sides of the column were the following legends: "1776. 1876. Now for 1976." "To the patrons of the Pico House, may you live 100 years." "No North, no South, no East, no West. A Fourth of July for all." "Independence Day. A welcome to all our guests." The entire front of the building was most gracefully festooned with wreaths of evergreens and long lines of miniature flags of the Union and of all nations. Directly opposite the Pico, the Oriental buildings were noticeable for their fine display, as were also the Fashion Stables.

Col. Wood's Opera House, attracted much attention by the tasty arrangements which its enterprising proprietors had made to show their full sympathy with the occasion.

Abbott's Theatre did the honors without stint, and displayed an unusual amount of bunting.

The Grand Central Hotel, by the unique and exceedingly attractive manner in which Messrs. Goss & Stackpole had arranged their contribution to the beautiful picture which the city presented, showed conclusively that they knew something else besides "how to keep a hotel." Thousands of flags streamed and fluttered on the front of the building, while from the roof of the building to the ground depended a number of ropes wrapped with the national colors, which had the appearance of storm stays and made the whole edifice look like a splendid ship crowding the waters under a press of parti-colored canvass.

Messrs. Salari & Whitney, of the St. Charles Hotel, spared neither pains nor expense in decorating their popular hostelrie. Starry banners waved profuse all over the building, and were arranged in squares and triangles, and other fanciful form, with such exceeding good taste that one could wish the handsome picture could remain a permanent institution.

The decorations of the Lafayette were confined principally to the balcony. A life-size portrait of Washington was encircled by flags and evergreens, and these were supplemented by other appliances of the decorative art in such a way as to produce a very pleasing effect.

The Farmers and Merchants' Bank did due honors to the occasion.

The City of Paris Dry Goods Store was noticeable for its tasty decorations.

Pete Thompson's retreat was fronted by a patriotic arch and evergreen embellishments.

The Fashion Saloon was embowered in a perfect wealth of evergreens, while a very pleasing effect was produced by innumerable flags and lanterns flashing and glowing among the verdure.

Ducommun's Block, one of the handsomest buildings in town, presented a very fine appearance.

The County Bank paid due regard to the anniversary.

The Commercial Bank building, especially the upper part of it in which are the offices of Goodall, Nelson & Perkins' line of steamships, Mr. C. Mc-Clellan, agent, presented a very attractive exterior.

Lanfranco Block was handsomely decorated, as were the stores and offices in the building.

Satter & Bayer exhibited admirable tact in their decorations, and the frontage to Congress Hall was picturesque with evergreens.

The United States Hotel, under the liberal hand of Messrs. Hammel and Denker, seemed transformed for the nonce into a suburban picnic ground. Two or three hundred forest trees, more or less, had been levied upon, by way of contribution, and these, adorned with flags and streamers, made up a cool, refreshing picture, which was by no means the least noticeable part of the general display.

The handsome residence and beautiful grounds of Mr. Morenhaut, the French Counsel, presented a delightful picture. The tri-color of France and stars and stripes of America were placed in harmonious juxtaposition, and over the door of the residence was the pleasant legend, "Friends since one hundred years."

On Spring street there were many notable displays. All the stores on Temple Block were gay with bunting, and the west front of the Court House was decorated with taste. From Court street to First the buildings were more or less handsomely trimmed, and the Mayor's office was a special point of admiration. On the opposite side of the street, Severance & Butler led off with a fine display of flags tastefully arranged; and the Star and Herald offices were gaudy with national colors. Post-Office Block, from balcony to sidewalk, was lavishly decorated, and from thence down to First there was no lack of tastefully arranged bunting for the eye to rest upon. Below First street, on both sides of Spring, a great number of private houses were gay with decorations, and so with the houses on Fort street and the intersecting thoroughfares.

Native and foreign born citizens vied with each other to make the day remarkable, and the rising generation of Los Angeles received a lesson in love of country which will last them through their lives. The observance of the day among business houses was not confined to Main street. Messrs. Mendel Meyer, Laventhal, M. W. Childs, Barrows, Furry & Co., S. C. Foy, the L. A. Social Club, Newmark & Co., Foster, Howard & Co., the Nortons, the National Guard Armory, Lips, Craigue & Co., Hellman, Haas & Co., the White House, Page, Gravel & Co., and many others did their share towards keeping up appearances.

The Southern Pacific Railroad Company and its agents and employees did the honors of the day very completely. The depot was handsomely decorated and the trains were rigged out in a holiday suit. The Wilmington train came thundering in with three or four hundred passengers, and the passenger cars and engine most beautifully adorned with flags and garlands of flowers. The engine of the Anaheim train was a marvel of decorative art and looked a perfect beauty. The Colton train joined in the general spirit of the day.

The L. A. & I. road was not behind in its observances. The depot was in gala attire, and the trains handsomely decked with patriotic colors.

PUBLIC DECORATIONS AND PROCESSION.

The prominent feature is the noble triple arch which spans Main street. The main span is thirty feet wide and thirty feet high; the side spans are

each seventeen fe t wide and twenty feet high.   The centre and side columns are four feet square and each about eight feet higher than the centre
of the arches.   Over the keystone of the centre arch is a fine statue of Columbia; on the two main columns respectivly are the statues of Washington, the
first President, and Grant, the present occupant of that exalted position.   On
the eastern column is a figure of one of "the boys in blue;" on the Western,
the statue of one of "the old Continentals."   Over the centre of each of the
side arches is a fine figure of the American eagle.   Under the statue of Columbia, on each side is the California coat of arms, and on each side of the
arches are the legends, "1776.   One hundred years ago.   1876."   Flags and
shields, the latter inscribed with the names of the States and of revolutionary
heroes, are disposed in well ordered series on the columns, and these are in
turn handsomely entwined with evergreen garlands.   The arch was the subject of universal compliments.   In addition to the above, Messrs. Lehman &
Co. stretched a large number of lines adorned with wreaths, flags and streamers across the principal streets.

The 38's Engine Company No. 1 set themselves to work regardless of
expense, to make the whereabouts of their place of business known.   They
erected a splendid triple arch in front of their house on Spring street, on the
keystone of the frame of which is a figure of a fireman in full dress with
trumpet in hand.   Underneath is a life size portrait of Washington surrounded with a wreath of laurel.   The legends, "The Centennial" and "Thirty-
Eight Fire Company," and any number of flags and shields bearing familiar
historical names adorn this fine structure, which is a noble tribute to the
public spirit of the boys of the 38's.

Confidence Engine Company No. 2 erected a fine bower of arches in
front of their building on Main street, which is a gem in its way.   Across
the street they stretched a line of evergreens and wreaths, from which de-
pends a splendid edition of "old glory" about forty feet long and of propor-
tionate width.   Although the two companies desire that their efforts should
be ranked among the public decorations, the entire expense has been borne
by them individually.

The Procession.

There were crowds of people coming into the city by car and carriage,
buggy and wagon.   They were coming on horseback and a-foot, and they
continued to come.   There were representatives by the score from all parts
of the county: Tustin City, Richland, Anaheim, Wilmington, Santa Monica,
San Fernando, Spadra—from all the four quarters of the compass, they came
and saw, rejoiced with us, hurrahed with us, were made welcome with us,
and we trust and believe went home well pleased with us.   The streets were
crowded at an early hour.   Every window along the line of march was
crowded, every balcony had its throng of eager lookers on.   There never
was such a crowd in the city before.   With one or two exceptions everybody
was on good behavior.   At an early hour the constituent part of the different divisions were seen hurrying to their places of rendezvous, and at the appointed hour the long line was set in motion and the march commenced.
The head of the column reached the corner of Temple street, and it was over
thirty minutes in passing that point.   The column was led by Major H. M.
Mitchell, Grand Marshal, assisted by his aids Capt. H. M. Smith, of Glassell,
Chapman & Smiths; Major E. M. Ross; J. A. Graves, Esq., of Brunson,
Eastman & Graves; and J. H. Howard, Esq., of San Gabriel.

Then came the Opera House Band, followed by the officers of the 1st
Division, Col. John F. Godfrey, Marshal; Messrs. M. S. Severance, A. G.
Walker, Wm. H. Stevens, and E. Germain, aids.   They were followed by the
Los Angeles Guard, Capt. Bailey commanding, and the Los Angeles Rifleros,
Capt. Pantalean commanding.   Next came the magnificent car appropriated
to the Goddess of Liberty, who was personated in a very queenly manner by
Miss Carrie Cohn.   She was attended by Miss Lulu Lehman, representing
Peace, and Miss Ally Carpenter, representing Plenty.

VETERANS OF THE MEXICAN WAR.

The Veterans of the Mexican War turned out strong, the following offi-cers and members appearing in the procession: Gen. Geo. Stoneman, Presi-dent; Peter Thompson, Wm. Todd,Vice-Presidents; J. D. Dunlap, Secretary; G. W. Whitehorn, Treasurer; Capt. Wm. Turner, Marshal; Thomas B.Wade, Assistant Marshal; Vincent Stenghter, W. B. Dunne, G. W. Whitehorn, R. T. Johnson, Trustees; J. V. Moore, T. J. Beebe, J. S. Griffin, H. W. Osborn, M. Halpin, W. C. Hughes, Jas. Thompson, J. O'Sullivan, A. W. Timms, M. Surrott, J. Knott, H. C. Millers, G. F. Wilson, J. A. Talbot, L. C. Goodwin, D. W. Alexander, Henry Hancock, S. C. Foster, C. Chaney, T. J. Ash, W. O. Baxter, J. R. W. Hand, E. Forbush, Job Roach, John Schumacher, J. P. Ryan, J. B. Caywood, J. Rossmore, Geo. Smith.

Next in order came the French Benevolent Society. A very beautiful feature of the splendid display made by our patriotic French fellow citizens was a triumphal chariot, elegantly adorned, in which were seated three young ladies, Miss Mary Lache, Miss Blanche Crowley and Miss Leonie Du-puytren. They represented the Goddess of Liberty, the second France and the third America. Their costumes were elegant and appropriate, and they constituted a very charming trio.

Carriages with the President of the Day, Orator, Poet,Chaplain and invi-ted guests followed, and then came the Marshal of the Second Division, Mr. Otto Von Ploennies, with his staff, consisting of Messrs. Hugo Done, F. Adam and F. Wolfhart.

The 38's followed. There were fifty men on the ropes and they looked splendidly. The Pioneers wore handsome blue caps and hats. The uniform of the 38's is a red shirt with blue hats. The hose carriage was covered with a blue canopy under which reclined Master George Kuhrts in uniform, as a representative of a hoseman. The steamer, fairly gleaming with a wealth of floral decorations, followed, drawn by six fine horses.

The hook and ladder truck, also very tastefully decorated, presented a very fine appearance, drawn by fifteen men in uniform.

Confidence Engine, No. 2, followed, drawn by six horses, richly compar-isoned in red, white and blue housings. A finely decorated canopy sur-mounted the splendidly trimmed steamer, in which Miss Emily Smith sat, personating America. Her costume was very rich and appropriate. The Pioneers of No. 2 wore red capes and black hats. The company uniform is blue shirt with silver facings, and a black hat. The boys made a grand ap-pearance.

A triumphal car upon which Confidence Engine Company seemed to have bestowed great pains, followed. It was covered by an ornamental can-opy beneath which sat Miss Hattie Furman, representing Columbia, and Miss Mamie Furman personating Uncle Sam; Henry Dockweiler, jr., an ex-empt fireman reclining on a coil of hose. At one corner of the canopy stood Master John Foster in the guise of "Mose," plug hat and all, at another, Master Harry Fanning as "Young Continental," in appropriate costume, at another, Master Willie Gard as the representative of the 38's, and at the oth-er, Master Isadore Dockweiler as one of the Confidence boys. Mrs. Gard and Miss Hattie Furman are entitled to credit for the excellent taste dis-played in the adornment of this beautiful car.

Wilmington hook and ladder truck followed and made a manly feature in the procession. The fire laddies may well be proud of their part in the grand procession.

The Junta Patriotica de Juarez and Turner rifles followed, making a very fine display. A number of carriages containing the Directors of the Junta Patriotica and private citizens followed, and the Third Division came in sight. This was led by Marshal Eugene Meyer and his aids, Messrs. James B. Lankershim, Brice McLellan, Aaron Smith and M. Clemente. This Division consisted of the following orders: Knights of Pythias, Indepen-dent Order of Odd Fellows, Improved Order of Red Men, Ancient Order of Hibernians, Irish Literary Society, and Irish Temperance Society. The general effect of this Division was excellent. The various orders turned out in force and presented a fine appearance. A pleasing feature of this Division was a car containing thirteen young Misses representing the thirteen original colonies.

The Fourth Division, Mr. F. Guirado and staff, now wheeled into line. The leading feature was the car of state, containing thirty-eight young ladies representing the States of the Union. The car was a triumph of decorative art and was hailed with cheers all along the line. The Butchers' Association, making a fine display, followed, and the inevitable forty-niners on their mules attracting their full share of attention, and half a dozen representatives of the noble red man of the forest, who, with their lay figure of Capt. Jack of the Modocs, contributed not a little to the hilarity of the occasion. Another handsome car containing a lad and girl in Continental times costumes, followed. It was occupied by Master Dan Richie as General George Washington, and Miss Mary Brown as Martha Washington. They attracted their full share of attention. The long line of trades display presented itself, preceded by a handsomely decorated wagon representing the Philadelphia Brewery.

Page & Gravel followed with an immense van in which a dozen or more artisans were plying the different branches of wagon making and blacksmithing. Page & Gravel never do anything by halves, and they made the most of their opportunity. The van was surmounted by a handsome picture representing Washington and other Revolutionary worthies welding the links of the Union chain. On each side of the wagon was this legend: "He who encourages home industry is a public benefactor. Mechanics—the foundation of civilization and progress. The American mechanic—the strength of the Union, the symbol of patriotism and the bone and sinew of the nation."

Next the Asbestine Stone Company with specimens of their excellent handiwork.

Then Cameron's display, comprising fish, flesh and fowl, and on the whole, unique and amusing.

Then a wagon with specimens of B. Aphodl's cooperage, with an immense wine vat marked "A. Pelanconi, wine dealer."

Then a fine display of Halliday's standard windmills.

Next a wagon from the Grange store laden with all sorts of toothsome delicacies. Then a laundry wagon driven by a lady, whose name we did not learn. Next came a fine display by the Adams Windmill Company. Then a wagon from Coulter & Harper's hardware store containing a little of everything in the housekeeping line from a stove to a nutmeg grater. Next came Trapp's fruit wagon with the motto, "Home Produce;" a good idea. Then Reinert's cooperage made a fine display with the legend, "Show us a leak in the Union and we will tighten it." W. M. Stoddard followed with a long line of wagons, carryalls and buggies. Then the Los Angeles Soap Company with specimens of their handiwork. Dotter & Bradley followed with a very handsome canopied wagon which contained a number of elegant specimens of their own manufacture of furniture. J. T. Woodward & Co., of the Los Angeles Broom Factory, made a very fine display of broom ware, all of which is manufactured in this city. The Centennial broom was a feature of the display. Next the New York Brewery, then the Los Angeles Steam Coffee Factory, and after them the Sewing Machine Companies. A long line of citizens on horseback and in carriages followed, and the most magnificent pageant that Los Angeles has ever witnessed came to an end as far as the passing of the procession was concerned. The names of the young ladies who assisted in the programme were:

Jennie Greenbaum, Lulu Lehman, Lulu Glassell, Rebecca Laventhal, Emma Newbauer, Hattie Newbaur, Hannah Cohen, Bertha Hellman, Alice Weil, Regina Prager, Lolita Dunne, Jennie Happ, Mary Goode, Florita Spiker, Matilda Johannsen, Laura Meyer, Hannah Laventhal, Lizzie Spencer, Fannie Hannah, Austina Mesmer, Ida Warren, Ella Warren, Emma Edwards, Anna Alexander, Johanna Williams, Sybel Foster, Francis Alexander, Lucy Williams, Jennie Stoddard, Therasa Heinsch, Rowena Scott, Aliza Anderson, Lizzie Weinsheank, Laura Hicks, Rose Raphael, Minnie Raphael, Fanny

Gerson, Ella Norton, Ceila Wilson, Mary Belle Scott, Mattie Cohen, Lizzie Chick, Lizzie Truman, Ella Seckler, Ally Carpenter, Ella Eaton, Louisa Lampke, Mary Morey, Stella Binford, Fanny Seebold, Milly Northal, Fannie Winbigler, Lilian Thatcher, Frances Karney, Emily McCarty, Minnie Nordholt, Delia O'Melveny, Monte Robarts, Julia Brair, Emily Fleishman, Ledia Smith, Bella Sepulveda, Nellie Smith, Nellie Bellow, Flora McPherson, Rose Kalisher, Kate Peeland, Fannie Richard, Maggie Davis, Anna Tulley, Emma Brain, Adela Brain, May L. Cumby, Lillie Clapp, Lulu Manor, Lelia Walters, Martha Heinch, Johanna Roeder, Sophia Magg, Conception Valdez.

The line of march, as laid down in the Programme, having been completed, the procession broke ranks at the Round House, and the Literary Exercises of the Day took place. Seats were prepared for about fifteen hundred people and they were all occupied, and hundreds listened throughout standing.

LITERARY EXERCISES.

After Hail Columbia by the band, General P. Banning, the President of the Day, introduced the Chaplain, Rev. Mr. Packard, who delivered a brief but impressive and appropriate prayer.

General Banning then delivered a short address replete with patriotic sentiments.

The hymn America was then sung by gentlemen from the different church choirs of the city.

Professor Thomas A. Saxon then read the Declaration of Independence, the performance of which is a somewhat ungracious task. His fine elocutionary powers were brought out.

The choir then sang Red, White and Blue.

The Poet of the Day, Mr. James J. Ayers, was then introduced to the audience, and he delivered the following

Centennial Poem.

Awake, my Muse! send forth thy latent fire,
  To sing a pæan to our country's name—
Let lofty thoughts thy swelling notes inspire,
  And flowing verse exalt her matchless fame.

Time, in his ceaseless march, has ushered in
  The year Centennial of our Nation's life;
And here, with bounding hopes, we now begin
  To grapple with the new-born cycle's strife.

The record of an hundred years is made;
  And, though with faults and errors it may teem,
Before its dazzling glories they will fade,
  As clouds disperse before Aurora's beam.

But, if the cycle past be fraught with blame,
  A mirror let it serve the cycle new,
And all the errors circled in its frame
  Monitions stand of evils to eschew.

E'en as where wrecks on sunken rocks are cast,
  Show watchful pilots courses safe to trace,
So we, by holding still in view the past,
  By Public Good may Public Ill replace.

One hundred years, summed in a nation's life,
  Form but the childhood term—the tender age—
When with disease and heedless error rife,
  The COMING MAN gropes through his infant stage.

Passed are all these; in manhood's stalwart pride,
  We sally forth with Destiny to cope,
And, daring, threatening winds and adverse tide,
  Launch on the world a new career of hope.

That hope is Freedom's here, and everywhere
  On this broad earth, where man, down trod,
Sends up to Heaven a supplicating prayer
  To shield him from the Tyrant's ruthless rod.

To us, entrusted by Almighty hand,
  The Ark of Freedom, which our fathers bore
In safety from the dread Oppressor's land,
  And planted on Columbia's Western shore—

To us is given the charge to guard it well;
  And if from Public Vice the danger come,
Insidious though it be, and, growing, swell
  With giant power, as erst in olden Rome,

Yet we will grapple with the monster's might—
  Place Virtue on our shields, and, with the spear
Of Truth, firm set in place, bend to the fight,
  And crush it under hoof, 'mid high career.

Freedom is ours in trust—oh, priceless trust!—
  To guard with hearts that beat the Godward side—
With souls that feel the impulse of the Just,
  And, rising, swell to Honor's manly pride!

In every votary's breast she rears a shrine,
  Where inward glows her quenchless vestal flame,
Enthroned she dwells in every patriot mind,
  And blazons forth from fields of deathless fame.

Out from thy pregnant womb, oh, Time! bring forth
  Men equal to our country's future needs,
With faces skyward, hearts of purest worth,
  And iron nerves strung to the bravest deeds.

With these, we'll bid defiance to the woes
  That Fate may launch against our hallowed land—
Unyielding breasts will brave our open foes,
  And Honor's foot on prostrate Baseness stand.

The band then played Yankee Doodle, after which Hon. James G. Eastman, the Orator of the Day, was introduced.

The Oration.

Mr. President and Fellow Citizens:—

As the sceptre was passing from the hands of the great Aztec monarch,
it was given him to see the future of this continent. The light of heaven's
prophecy shone upon him, and, melting the shackles of superstition, enabled
him, through the vista of years, to see such a government as ours. He said:
"The long, long cycles pass away; an age of battles intervenes, and, lo! there
is a government whose motto is, 'Freedom and God!' Those words are dark
to my understanding, but pass them down from generation to generation as
a sacred tradition; for some time, with this motto, the people of this continent will take their place among the deathless nations of the earth."

We are to-day celebrating the one-hundredth anniversary of the realiza-
ion of Montezuma's prophecy. I congratulate you upon its advent; the aus-
picious omens which greeted its coming and welcome its presence.

It is well, in such an age of secular toil and struggle, that each year
should bring one day when the din of the marts is hushed; when the jostle
and strife of commerce cease; when the anvil is silent and the workshop
dumb; when the money changers desert the temple and the miser's ears lis-
ten to a music sweeter than the music of his worshipped gold; when secta-
rian strife and partisan bickerings retire shame-faced before the presence of
that broader patriotism, that feeling of universal brotherhood, which fills
every American heart and mind with the thoughts of our country. It is well

that there comes one day when the student and the laborer, the banker and the pauper, losing sight of all distinctions of fortune and chance, can meet on common ground and, in the full enjoyment of a common sovereignty, walk hand in hand—proud, exultant, thoughtful, admiring—through these galleries of civil greatness; when we may own together the spell of one hour of our history upon us all; when we may rise into the sphere of a higher life in the contemplation of a government founded upon equality, anchored in the patriotism of all its citizens, aiming at the greatest good for all, and in grateful homage bow before the throne Divine, and mingle forty million voices in one common prayer that Columbia may remain the favored child of Heaven, and that peace be within her gates and joy within her palaces forever.

While, since the earliest governmental organization, all nations have had their festal hours and days of rejoicing; yet, sir, it seems to me, no people in the commemoration of an event were ever surrounded by circumstances of such a universal character to contribute to their just and proper exultation as the American people this day. It is the world's jubilee! Wherever civilization has written the record of its advancement, wherever love of freedom has warmed a human heart, the dawning of this sacred anniversary is greeted with feelings of universal joy and gratitude.

In every port and in every civilized city; beneath the shadow of St. Peter's and the Brahmin temple; over the sepulchres at Athens, and the palace at Yeddo, to-day the sacred emblem of our nationality, that ensign of freedom, that type of human progress, that glorious tri-colored banner,

"Whose crimson by courage was pictured,
  Whose white is from purity true,
  O'er which love spread a halo of beauty
  In a star-lighted heaven of blue,"

Waves in triumphant grandeur, the joy, the pride, the protection of the civilized world.

Within the sound of the old bell, beneath the shadow of the old hall where one hundred years ago a nation was born, are assembled to-day representatives from all the world to behold our offerings to its history. And what do we give one hundred years of intellectual freedom; a century of equal rights?

And, sir, when I contemplate the grandeur of this anniversary—that each returning year for a century it has been the occasion for the efforts of our most learned, wise and eloquent; that the theme itself is nothing less than universal liberty; that the principles giving value to the event we commemorate gave new life to the world, a new impetus to human progress; and that the rejoicing over their general recognition has swelled into a mighty chorus, chanted in every clime—I feel a delicacy in attempting to say aught which shall be appropriate. I feel the spell of an unbound grandeur, which comes with the day, rides upon the sunlight, sparkles in the rippling wave, paints its presence in a beauteous picture on the very brow of nature, and which, though felt by all, by none can be described. It makes silence eloquent.

The reverberating tones of the bell which one hundred years ago to-day proclaimed the birth of a new nation—the realization of a hope which led the children of the Lord from Egypt—gave Thermopylæ to history, and freedom to mankind, shall resound through the corridors of time when the landmarks of history shall have passed away.

When the mournful zephyrs, passing the plain where Marathon once stood, shall find no mound to kiss; when the arch of Titus shall have been obliterated; the Collosseum crumbled into antique dust; the greatness of Athens degenerated into dim tradition; Alexander, Cæsar and Napoleon forgotten; the memories of Independence Hall shall still bloom in imperishable freshness.

In the wreck of matter, two events shall stand forth in immortal youth: the crucifixion and the American Declaration; the birth of the doctrine of universal love, and universal liberty.

But, sir, while the theme is so comprehensive that no human mind can grasp its fullness, or picture its glories, there is yet a fitness and wisdom in

our meeting and communing. We cannot but be benefitted by a contemplation of the greatness of the inauguration of which this day commemorates,
and a thoughtful resume of the duties which devolve upon us as citizens of a
land so signally favored. It will not prove unprofitable to us to pause, if not
once a year, at least once in a century, and thoughtfully review the track o'er
which American greatness has trod, the school in which it has been educated, the crucible in which it has been sublimated.

When we wander back in patriotic piety to that lone rock of Plymouth,
where, beneath a frowning sky, and witnessed by the wild, fierce, wintry
grandeur of the wilderness, the germ of our government was planted,and
to-day behold that government laying its hands upon two oceans, upheld by
the strong arm of nearly fifty million people, commanding and receiving the
loyal homage of a continent, and the profound respect of the universal world,
we can scarcely comprehend the wonderful trasition.

And yet, sir, this great consummation is not the work of chance, nor this
great model specimen of govermental architecture the result of magic. No;
it is born of legitimate cause. This great growth,great development, great progress, great advancement,annihilating wildernesses,spanning rivers, girding a
continent with steel, is the result of fixed, immutable laws, and has been
brought about by means which could not fail of such an end. And, sir, in
the contemplation of those great casual facts we may read the lesson which
this day with its memories should inculcate; that we ourselves have a duty
to perform in connection with this great work; and that this heritage of freedom, this mighty government of protection, this lovely land of peace and
progress, is not an inheritance entailed upon us and our posterity which may
not be defeated; that we are not to stand as mere, awe-stricken admirers and
enjoyers of this product of the labor of past generations, wondering how long
the splendid scene will last, and the great protecting arch of liberty stand, but
realize that we are links in the great chain, wheels in this monster machine,
active makers of the glory of this Republic, and responsible alike to the past
and future for the manner in which we study and perform our part.

It is plainly evident to any candid reviewer of the work of our fathers
that it was their earnest aim and intention to found a government based upon
the active participating consent of the governed. A government whose sovereignty should be perpetual because its power was equally distributed among
all who enjoyed its benefits. A government in which the rights of all would
be respected and protected, because the power and remedy were placed equally
in the hands of all. A government which would be strong because it was to
the interest of all to make it strong. A government that should be progress-
ive, in that, all being equal, it must keep pace with the progress of all. And
sir, there was much to impel them to the establishment of such a system.—
They had become the hereditary victims of a mighty oppression; they were
the descendants and representatives of those who for centuries had felt and
experienced the evils of the prevailing forms of government, and the necessity of a new form and system avoiding the errors of the old. They had learned, either by direct experience, or immediate tradition, that in the existing
forms, power was not only hereditary, but was righteousness, and that freedom of thought was dependent upon the accident of birth.

Throughout the ages, the "mills of God," which 'tis said grind slow but
yet exceeding small, had been grinding out this grist which culminated in a
government based upon the equal rights and equal will of the governed.

It was the legitimate tendency of such causes to produce such effects.
The evil which had hitherto existed was the concentration of power in the
hands of the few. The remedy adopted was a universal distribution of power among the governed. In short, from the time of the promulgation of the
American Declaration, and the laying of the foundation of the American system, the universal right of equality,—the innate dignity of man, and the sov-
ereignity of the people, have been recognized.

This creed, so broad and grand, planted the colonies, led them through
the desert and sea of ante-revolutionary life; railled them all together to resist the attacks of a king and minister; sharpened and pointed the bayonets
of all their battles; strengthened their sword arms, and gave fatal aim to their

bullets; burst forth from a million lips; beamed in a million eyes, sounded out in the revolutionary eloquence of fire; awoke the thunder and gleamed in the lightning of the deathless words of Otis, Henry and Adams; survived the excitement of war, and the necessities of order; penetrated and tinged all our constitutional composition and policy, and all our party organization, and stands to-day radiant and defiant upon the summit of our greatcess—the authoritative proclamation of freedom to humanity.

And this thought sir, is worth nothing only as it leads us to a contemplation of the correlative duties which must follow, and a realization of our joint and individual responsibility to humanity and God for the progress, the perpetuation and the success of this greatest of human experiments.. It is to an appreciation of that duty—its exalted sublimity—its o'crwecning importance—its high responsibility—that the memories which are borne upon the golden sunbeams of this anniversary should lead us—to the contemplation of this great trust direct us. It must be evident to all who give the subject thought, that a great portion of the American people have never arrived at a proper estimate of the sublimity of their political eminence, of their responsibility for the disasters which have shadowed the march of our national progress. We are apt, in the age of excitement, of struggles for wealth, of false social rules and systems, and of poisoned ambition, to lose sight of our own sovereignty and its incidents. We see those who, by nefarious practises, aided by our own indifference, have reached places of official eminence, wasting the wealth of the nation, the time belonging to their constituents, destroying the credit of the Government, prostituting the dignity of their power to the furtherance of measures which are portentous of evil and pregnant with calamity.

We murmur and complain, give loud utterance to our momentary indignation, and then turn to our individual avocations as if we were impotent to avert the evil, powerless to resist the cyclone of disaster, as if we had no responsibility in the matter. Is this a proper exercise of our boasted sovereignty? Is this the discharge of a duty we owe to a government whose very life, and our protection under it, depend upon the active, thoughtful participation of each of its citizens? Are we thereby paying for the great benefits we have received? Are we keeping faith with the past, or maintaining our integrity with the future? Is it not rather our duty to call those public officers to account, and make of them such an example that none will dare repeat the experiment? Why not arraign these mighty criminals before the bar of public opinion, and by their utter condemnation and discomfiture stay the progress of this mighty evil?

I look upon it, sir, as the first duty of an American citizen to ascertain his political obligations to his country and faithfully and religiously discharge them. He should feel as if the right of suffrage depended upon its exercise, and never fail in the latter until he is willing to surrender the former. He should actively contribute to the formation and preservation of an elevated, pure public sentiment, which shall cause peculation, duplicity, demagogueism and political corruption to retreat shame-faced from its presence.

We may not excuse ourselves upon the plea of ignorance of public affairs. Basking in the sunlight of perfect freedom, sitting beneath the shadow of universities, visited daily, yea, almost hourly by the messengers of literature and news, receiving by the harnessed lightning record of every heart-throb of the nation, and every shock to any nerve in the great system—we are not ignorant, we cannot be ignorant; nor can we by such a plea deceive the world or ourselves, nor lull our conscience to sleep.

We owe it not alone to the past and future, but to our own age, its mighty progress, its glorious history, its wonderful triumphs, its past promise to know and do.

There is, sir, to my mind, another duty of great magnitude which we should carefully consider and faithfully discharge, and the neglect of which threatens the most disastrous consequences. I refer to the necessity of protecting ourselves from the contaminating influence of political and moral skepticism, resulting from the immigration hither and settlement in our midst of those who believe in no government but a despotism, and no moral obligation beyond fealty to a monarch.

There are, sir, those who think the expansive power of this government is nearly exhausted, and that our invitation to the people of every clime to join in our great enterprise and participate in the work of glory our fathers inaugurated should be withdrawn. This is in part true, in part false. Our present greatness as a nation is attributable to the mixed elements of worth which the fascination of our theory has drawn from the world. It has ever been the better class, viewed governmentally, that has severed the ties of home and nationality to lay the offering of future life and toil as a tribute to the theory of a government absolutely free and equal in that it gave every man an opportunity to make himself the equal of every man.

The ingenious Swiss, the practical Englishman, the polished Frenchman, the philosohic German, the gallant Spaniard, the busy, country-loving Irishman, and the sturdy Swede, bringing the peculiar characteristics of climate, birth, education, skill and surroundings, and a devoted admiration of our governmental system, have by constant admixture become the common parents of the American of to-day. To all such the theory is false. To them and their descendants, now and forever, and to all who come with brain or muscle or skill to enjoy the blessings of our government because they believe in its principles and love its doctrines, and desire to contribute to its success, the invitation is irrevocable, and the doors are forever open. They are brothers in blood, in thought, in aspiration and inheritance,

But, sir, there is another class, with regard to which this theory is true. There is a pagan element, wedded to monarchy, devoted to idolatry, despising our institutions, hating our civilization, spitting upon our social system, laughing at our patriotism, preying upon our substance, and demoralizing our people, against whom the gates should be at once and for all time closed. This grand continent, with its civilization and wondrous development, its cultivated valleys and happy homes, is not the lap into which China may spew its criminals and paupers, its invalids and idiots, its surplus moral and physical leprosy. Now, at once, in a manner respecting all law, and becoming the dignity of a great nation, must they be made to understand, not only that their presence is unwelcome, but that their further immigration will not be tolerated. Let the world to-day know that none are entitled to permanent seats in the temple of liberty who are not willing communicants at her altar. The duties devolving upon an American citizen who would live up to the fulness of his privilege are manifold, and I may not pause, and in this brief hour attempt their enumeration. I may not stop to consider how every citizen, directly or indirectly, regardless of vocation or station, is intimately connected with and exercises his influence upon all that is useful, grand and good. We all feel that every triumph of art, of science or of literature which is achieved under the broad liberality of the American system, is a triumph in which we are all participants—a glory in which we are all contributors.

But, sir, there is one duty of such paramount importance that I cannot pass it by. The late unhappy struggle which shook our continent, the years of blood, the desolated homes, new-made graves, cold, white monuments, bleaching, uncovered bones, those sad, sad pages of our history, have tended to bring it into bold relief, and it is meet, fitting and proper that upon this day we should, around our country's century-christened altar, pledge our faith to its performance. I refer to the duty of establishing and maintaining a more exalted standard of American nationality—a more comprehensive brotherhood—a more universal love. Have we not been negligent in the cultivation of that near acquaintance which alone can bind, unite and cement a nation? Wooed by different influences, lost in local individuality, we became sectionalized, and allowed those words, disastrous to our peace and destructive of our harmony—North, South, East and West—to creep into our vocabulary and be spoken in our national councils. Yielding to local rather than national interests, local rather than national traditions, we became alienated, and our alienation resulted in the bloodiest war of history, threatening the overthrow of our government and the final downfall of Republican institusons. We may learn from this sorrowful chapter the necessity of more intimate relations, the cultivation of a more national and united aspiration, a feeling of more perfect oneness, that our government is our common mother. Let us fully realize that our greatness is dependent upon our harmony, and make sacrifice of all that will imperil our national growth or our national liberty.

And, sir, in our system of education we must endeavor to inculcate a broad and statesmanlike intelligence and faith. We must not educate simply in art, science, mechanism, or social and classic literature, but in the science of government, the meaning of our constitution, the importance of its perpetuity, the concessions and compromises born of charity and incident to a Democratic form of government. We must teach our children, and learn ourselves that sectional words or feeling can have no place in the treatment of national questions. But that the preservation and good of the whole country must be the keystone of all systems of national policy. Let us, upon this sacred occasion, visit in fancy the graves of our great statesmen who have left the record of a life's devotion to America, and all of America. Who, loving home and their immediate constituents, yet, when the ark of our safety was imperiled, ever rose to the true dignity of American statesmanship and counseled for all, yea, for all; and let us return robed in the mantle of their patriotism.

I thank God that to-day, around the birthplace of American liberty, the brave and war-stained of every State and Territory, burying their differences and mistakes, leaving under the shadow of the laurel and the willow their sorrows and their dead, are marching hand in hand, with one heart, one hope, one flag and one destiny.

Sir, the day might be spent in discussing the duties which its memories bring, but I forbear. I have endeavored to speak of the more important ones and avoid the pollution of an hour so sacred by a display of rhetoric or idle words. And if, when the sun, kissing the night and sinking to rest upon its bosom, lulled by the murmuring waves of our own mighty ocean, shall close the history of this day, we shall have been drawn in any one respect nearer the fountain of political truth, or been impelled to more firmly resolve to do our own duty and our whole duty as citizens, then our meeting and celebration will not have been in vain.

Sir, we are now a great people, standing at the head of the governments of the world. Our navy floats in every water; in all progress that characterizes civilization we bow to none. In all that tends to make a nation great, we have made a glorious history. True, some of its pages bear the stain of tears and blood, and evidence of our follies finds a place upon the record, yet it is grand as human record ever has been, and if we profit by the lessons our follies have taught us, devote our lives and intelligence to the establishment of a higher nationaltity, a broader patriotism, a more self-sacrificing devotion to our common country, when, in another century, our children's children shall meet to celebrate our governmental birth, America shall be the pride and boast of the free, the Queen of the earth.

And when, upon the last day, before the great Founder and Ruler of all governments, the nations of the earth are summoned to bring the record of their stewardship—when England shall come with offerings of manufactures, her commerce and her proud statesmanship; France, with her centuries of refinement; her proud achievements in letters, wit, thought and science; Spain with her conquests and song; Germany with her broad philosophy, grand poetry and wondrous learning; Italy with her ages of music and art; America, robed in equal rights, radiant with universal love and liberty, shall approach the throne Divine, and depositing as her offering the trophies of peace and the benedictions of mankind, shall be crowned with the approval of the Everlasting God!

At the conclusion of Mr. Eastman's magnificent effort, which was listened to with rapt attention throughout, the audience burst out in a roar of enthusiastic applause.

After Mr. Eastman, the President of the Day introduced Mr. Morenhaut, the venerable French Consul of Los Angeles, who delivered, in a very low tone, however, some appropriate remarks in reference to the Revolutionary era of our country and the distinguished part France took with us in our infant struggle.

Rev. Mr. Edelman was then introduced, and delivered the benediction, which closed the exercises.

————0————

NOTE.

The heading of Chapter I. should read to January, 1847, instead of August, 1846.

Chapter I. was prepared by J. J. WARNER.

Chapter II. by BENJAMIN HAYES.

Chapter III. by DOCTOR J. P. WIDNEY.

AN

HISTORICAL SKETCH

— OF —

LOS ANGELES COUNTY,

CALIFORNIA.

✢

From the Spanish occupancy, by the Founding of the Mission San Gabriel Archangel, September 8, 1771, to July 4, 1876.

✢

PUBLISHED BY

LOUIS LEWIN & Co.,

No 14 SPRING STREET.

1876.

Mirror Printing, Ruling and Binding House, Los Angeles, Cal.